DANIEL IN THE Critics' DEN

DANIEL IN THE *Critics'* DEN

A Defense of the Historicity of the Book of Daniel

Sir Robert Anderson

KREGEL PUBLICATIONS
Grand Rapids, Michigan 49501

Daniel in the Critics' Den, by Sir Robert Anderson. Published in 1990 by Kregel Publications, a division of Kregel, Inc. P. O. Box 2607, Grand Rapids, MI 49501. All rights reserved.

Library of Congress Cataloging-in-Publication Data

Anderson, Robert, Sir, 1841-1918.
  Daniel in the critics' den / Sir Robert Anderson.

  Reprint. Originally published: 3rd ed. London:
J. Nisbet, 1909.
  Includes Index.

  1. Bible. O.T. Daniel—Criticism, interpretation, etc.
I. Title.

BS1555.A6   1990   224'.506—dc20   90-4683
                                           CIP
ISBN   0-8254-2133-0 (pbk.)

        2 3 4 5 Printing/Year 94 93

Contents

Preface

ALTHOUGH this volume appears under an old title, it is practically a new work. The title remains, lest any who possess my " Reply to Dean Farrar's *Book of Daniel*" should feel aggrieved on finding part of that treatise reproduced under a new designation.[1] But the latter half of this book is new; and the whole has been recast, in view of its main purpose and aim as a reply to Professor Driver's Commentary in "The Cambridge Bible" series.

The appearance of Professor Driver's *Book of Daniel* marks an epoch in the Daniel controversy. Hitherto there has been no work in existence which English exponents of the sceptical hypothesis would accept as

---

[1] It appeared first as an article in *Blackwood's Magazine*, and afterwards separately in book form.

a fair and adequate expression of their views. But now the oracle has spoken. The most trusted champion of the Higher Criticism in England has formulated the case against the Book of Daniel; and if that case can be refuted—if it can be shown that its apparent force depends on a skilful presentation of doubtful evidence upon the one side, to the exclusion of overwhelmingly cogent evidence upon the other—the result ought to be an "end of controversy" on the whole question.

It rests with others to decide whether this result is established in the following pages. I am willing to stake it upon the issues specified in Chapter VII. And even if the reader should see fit to make that chapter the starting-point of his perusal of my book, I am still prepared to claim his verdict in favour of Daniel.

And here I should premise, what will be found more than once repeated in the sequel, that the inquiry involved in the

Daniel controversy is essentially judicial. An experienced Judge with an intelligent jury—any tribunal, indeed, accustomed to sift and weigh conflicting testimony—would be better fitted to deal with it than a company of all the philologists of Christendom. The philologist's proper place is in the witness-chair. He can supply but a part, and that by no means the most important part, of the necessary evidence. And if a single well-ascertained fact be inconsistent with his theories, the fact must prevail. But this the specialist is proverbially slow to recognise. He is always apt to exaggerate the importance of his own testimony, and to betray impatience when evidence of another kind is allowed legitimate weight. And nowhere is this tendency more marked than among the critics.

In the preface to his *Continuity of Scripture*, Lord Hatherley speaks of "the supposed evidence on which are based some **very** confident assertions of a self-styled 'higher criticism.'" And he adds, "Assuming the learning to be profound and accurate which has collected the material for much critical performance, the logic by which conclusions are deduced from those materials is frequently grievously at fault, and open to the judgment of all who may have been accustomed to sift and weigh evidence." My apology for this book is that I can claim a humble place in the category described in these concluding words. Long accustomed to deal with evidence in difficult and intricate inquiries, I have set myself to investigate the genuineness of the Book of Daniel, and the results of my inquiry are here recorded.

Lord Hatherley was not the only Lord Chancellor of our time to whom earnest thought and study brought a settled conviction of the Divine authority and absolute integrity of Holy Scripture. The two very great men who in turn succeeded him in that high office, though versed in the literature of the critics, held unflinchingly to the same conclusion. And while some, perhaps, would dismiss the judgment of men like Lord Cairns and Lord Selborne as being that of "mere laymen," sensible people the whole world over would accept their decision upon an intricate judicial question of this kind against that of all the pundits of Christendom.

As regards my attitude towards criticism, I deprecate being misunderstood. Every book I have written gives proof of fearlessness in applying critical methods to the study of the Bible. But the Higher Criticism is a mere travesty of all true criticism. Secular writers are presumed to be trustworthy unless reason is found to discredit their testimony. But the Higher Criticism starts with the assumption that everything in Scripture needs to be confirmed by external evidence. It reeks of its evil origin in German infidelity. My indictment of it, therefore, is not that it is criticism, but that it is criticism of a low and spurious type, akin to that for which the baser sort of "Old Bailey" practitioner is famed. True criticism seeks to elucidate the truth: the Higher Criticism aims at establishing pre-judged results. And in exposing such a system the present volume has an import-ance far beyond the special subject of which it treats.

A single instance will suffice. The "An-nalistic tablet" of Cyrus, which records his conquest of Babylon, is received by the critics as Gospel truth, albeit the deception which underlies it would be clear even to a clever schoolboy. But even as read by the critics it affords confirmation of Daniel which is startling in its definiteness in regard to Belshazzar and Darius the Mede. It tells us that the capture of the inner city was marked by the death of Belshazzar, or (as the inscription calls him throughout) "the son of the king." And further, we learn from it that Cyrus's triumph was shared by a Median of such note that his name was united with his own in the proclamation of an amnesty. And yet so fixed is the determination of the critics to discredit the Book of Daniel, that all this is ignored.

The inadequacy of the reasons put forward for rejecting Daniel clearly indicate that there is some potent reason of another kind in the background. It was the miraculous element in the book that set the whole pack of foreign sceptics in full cry. In this age of a silent heaven such men will not tolerate the idea that God ever intervened directly in the affairs of men. But this is too large a subject for incidental treatment. I have dealt with it in *The Silence of God*, and I would refer specially to Chapter III. of that work.

Other incidental questions involved in the controversy I have treated of here; but as they are incidental, I have relegated them to the Appendix. And if any one claims a fuller discussion of them, I must ask leave to refer to the work alluded to by Professor Driver in his *Book of Daniel*—namely, *The Coming Prince, or The Seventy Weeks of Daniel.*

R. A.

Preface to the Third Edition

MOST of the "historical errors" in Daniel, which Professor Driver has copied from Bertholdt's work of a century ago, have been disposed of by the erudition and research of our own day. But the identity of Darius the Mede has been referred to in former editions of the present work as an unsolved historical difficulty in the Daniel controversy. That question, however, seems to be settled by a verse in Ezra, which has hitherto been used only by Voltaire and others to discredit the Prophet's narrative.

Ezra records that in the reign of Darius Hystaspis the Jews presented a petition to

the King, in which they recited Cyrus' decree
authorising the rebuilding of their Temple.
The wording of the petition clearly indicates
that, to the knowledge of the Jewish leaders,
the decree in question had been filed in
the house of the archives in Babylon. But
the search there made for it proved fruit-
less, and it was ultimately found at Ecbatana
(or Achmetha: Ezra vi. 2). How, then,
could a State paper of this kind have been
transferred to the Median capital?

The only reasonable explanation of this
extraordinary fact completes the proof that
the vassal king whom Daniel calls Darius was
the Median general, Gobryas (or Gubaru),
who led the army of Cyrus to Babylon. As
noticed in these pages (163, 165, *post*), the
testimony of the inscriptions points to that
conclusion. After the taking of the city,
his name was coupled with that of Cyrus in
proclaiming an amnesty. And he it was who
appointed the governors or prefects; which
appointments Daniel states were made by

Darius. The fact that he was a prince of the royal house of Media, and presumably well known to Cyrus, who had resided at the Median Court, would account for his being held in such high honour. He had governed Media as Viceroy when that country was reduced to the status of a province; and to any one accustomed to deal with evidence, the inference will seem natural that, for some reason or other, he was sent back to his provincial throne, and that, in returning to Ecbatana, he carried with him the archives of his brief reign in Babylon.

I will only add that the confusion and error which the "Higher Critics" attribute to the sacred writers are mainly due to their own failure to distinguish between the several judgments of the era of the exile—the "Servitude," the "Captivity," and the "Desolations" (Jer. xxix. 10; 2 Chron. xxxvi. 21. See pp. 112, 117–119, *post*).

R. A.

1

The "Higher Criticism," and Dean Farrar's Estimate of the Bible

By "all people of discernment" the "Higher Criticism" is now held in the greatest repute. And discernment is a quality for which the dullest of men are keen to claim credit. It may safely be assumed that not one person in a score of those who eagerly disclaim belief in the visions of Daniel has ever seriously considered the question. The literature upon the subject is but dull reading at best, and the inquiry demands a combination of qualities which is comparatively rare. A newspaper review of some ponderous treatise, or a frothy discourse by some popular preacher, will satisfy most men. The German literature upon the controversy they know nothing of, and the erudite writings of scholars are by no means to their taste, and probably beyond their capacity. Dean Farrar's *Book of Daniel* therefore meets a much-felt want. Ignored by scholars it certainly will be, and the majority of serious theologians will deplore it; but it supplies "the man in the street" with a reason for the unfaith that is in him.

The narrowness with which it emphasises everything that either erudition or ignorance can urge upon one side of a great controversy, to the exclusion of the rest, will relieve him from the irksome task of thinking out the problem for himself; and its pedantry is veiled by rhetoric of a type which will admirably suit him. He cannot fail to be deeply impressed by "the acervation of endless conjectures," and "the unconsciously disingenuous resourcefulness of traditional harmonics." His acquaintance with the unseen world will be enlarged by discovering that Gabriel, who appeared to the prophet, is "the archangel";[1] and by

---

[1] P. 275.

learning that "it is only after the Exile that we find angels and demons playing a more prominent part than before, divided into classes, and even marked out by special names."[1] It is not easy to decide whether this statement is the more astonishing when examined as a specimen of English, or when regarded as a dictum to guide us in the study of Scripture. But all this relates only to the form of the book. When we come to consider its substance, the spirit which pervades it, and the results to which it leads, a sense of distress and shame will commingle with our amazement.

What the dissecting-room is to the physician criticism is to the theologian. In its proper sphere it is most valuable; and it has made large additions to our knowledge of the Bible. But it demands not only skill and care, but reverence; and if these be wanting, it cannot fail to be mischievous. A man of the baser sort may become so degraded by the use of the surgeon's knife that he loses all respect for the body of

---

[1] P. 191.

his patient, and the sick-room is to him but the antechamber to the mortuary. And can we with impunity forget the reverence that is due to "the living and eternally abiding word of God"?[1]

It behoves us to distinguish between true criticism as a means to clear away from that word corruptions and excrescences, and to gain a more intelligent appreciation of its mysteries, and the Higher Criticism as a rationalistic and anti-christian crusade. The end and aim of this movement is to eliminate God from the Bible. It was the impure growth of the scepticism which well-nigh swamped the religious life of Germany in the eighteenth century.

Eichhorn set himself to account for the miracles of Scripture. The poetic warmth of oriental thought and language sufficed, in his judgment, to explain them. The writers wrote as they were accustomed to think, leaving out of view all second causes, and attributing results immediately to God. This theory had its day. It obtained enthusiastic

---

[1] 1 Pet. i. 23.

acceptance for a time. But rival hypotheses were put forward to dispute its sway, and at last it was discarded in favour of the system with which the name of De Wette is prominently associated. The sacred writers were honest and true, but their teaching was based, not upon personal knowledge, still less upon divine inspiration, but upon ancient authorities by which they were misled. Their errors were due to the excessive literalness with which they accepted as facts the legends of earlier days. De Wette, like Eichhorn, desired to rescue the Bible from the reproach which had fallen upon it. Upon them at least the halo of departed truth still rested. But others were restrained by no such influence. With the ignorance of Pagans and the animus of apostates they perverted the Scriptures and tore them to pieces.

One of the old Psalms,[1] in lamenting with exquisite sadness the ruin brought by the heathen upon the holy city and land, declares that fame was apportioned according to zeal

---

[1] Ps. lxxiv.

and success in the work of destruction. A
like spirit has animated the host of the
critics. It is a distressing and baneful
ordeal to find oneself in the company of
those who have no belief in the virtue of
women. The mind thus poisoned learns to
regard with suspicion the purest inmates of
a pure home. And a too close familiarity
with the vile literature of the sceptics leads
to a kindred distrust of all that is true and
holy in our most true and holy faith. Every
chapter of this book gives proof to what
an extent its author has suffered this moral
and spiritual deterioration ; and no one can
accept its teaching without sinking, imper-
ceptibly it may be, but surely and inevitably,
to the same level. Kuenen, one of the
worst of the foreign sceptics, is Dean Farrar's master and guide in the interpretation
of Daniel. And the result is that he revels
in puerilities and extravagances of exegesis
and criticism which the best of our British
contemporary scholars are careful to re-
pudiate.

The Book of Daniel is not "the work of

a prophet in the Exile" (if indeed such a personage as Daniel ever really existed), "but of some faithful *Chasid* in the days of the Seleucid tyrant."[1] Its pretended miracles are but moral fables. Its history is but idle legend, abounding in "violent errors" of the grossest kind.[2] Its so-called predictions alone are accurate, because they were but the record of recent or contemporary events. But Dr. Farrar will not tolerate a word of blame upon "the holy and gifted Jew"[3] who wrote it. No thought of deceiving any one ever crossed his mind.[4] The reproach which has been heaped upon him has been wholly owing to Jewish arrogance and Christian stupidity in misreading his charming and elevating romance. For it is not only fiction, but "*avowed* fiction,"[5] and was never meant to be regarded in any other light. In a word, the book is nothing more than a religious novel, differing from other kindred works only in its venerable antiquity and the multiplicity of its blunders.

[1] P. 118.   [2] P. 45.
[3] P. 119.   [4] Pp. 43, 85.   [5] P. 43.

Accepting these results, then, what action shall we take upon them? In proportion surely to our appreciation of the preciousness of Holy Scripture, shall be our resoluteness in tearing the Book of Daniel from its place in the sacred canon, and relegating it to the same shelf with *Bel and the Dragon* and *The Story of Susanna*. By no means. Dr. Farrar will stay our hand by the assurance that—

"Those results . . . are in no way derogatory to the preciousness of this Old Testament Apocalypse." "No words of mine," he declares, "can exaggerate the value which I attach to this part of our Canonical Scriptures. . . . Its right to a place in the Canon is undisputed and indisputable, and there is scarcely a single book of the Old Testament which can be made more richly 'profitable for teaching, for reproof, for correction, for instruction in righteousness: that the man of God may be complete, completely furnished unto every good work.'" [1]

-----

[1] P. 4. Again and again throughout this volume the author uses like words in praise of the Book of Daniel. Here are a few of them: "It is indeed a noble book, full of glorious lessons" (p. 36). "Its high worth and canonical authority" (p. 37). "So far from undervaluing its teaching, I have always been strongly drawn to this book of

Christian writers who find reason to reject one portion of the sacred canon or another are usually eager to insist that in doing so they increase the authority and enhance the value of the rest. It has remained for the Dean of Canterbury, in impugning the Book of Daniel, to insult and degrade the Bible as a whole. An expert examines for me the contents of my purse. I spread out nine-and-thirty sovereigns upon the table, and after close inspection he marks out one as a counterfeit. As I console myself for the loss by the deepened confidence I feel that all the rest are sterling coin, he checks me by the assurance that there is scarcely a single one of them which is any better. The Book of Daniel is nothing more than a religious novel, and it teems with errors on every page, and yet we are gravely told that of all the thirty-nine books

---

Scripture" (p. 37). "We acknowledge the canonicity of the book, its high value when rightly apprehended, and its rightful acceptance as a sacred book" (p. 90). And most wonderful of all, at p. 118 the author declares that, in exposing it as a work of fiction, "We add to its real value" !

of the Old Testament there is *scarcely a single book* which is of any higher worth! The expert's estimate of the value of my coins is clear. No less obvious is Dr. Farrar's estimate of the value of the books of the Bible.

It is precisely this element which renders this volume so pernicious. The apostle declares that " Every Scripture *inspired of God* is also profitable for teaching, for reproof, for correction, for instruction in righteousness: that the man of God may be complete, furnished completely unto every good work ; " [1]

---

[1] 2 Tim. iii. 16. I quote the R.V. because it gives more unequivocal testimony to the inspiration of Scripture than does the A.V. According to the A.V. the apostle asserts that all Scripture is inspired of God : according to the R.V. he assumes this as a truth which does not need even to be asserted. For " every Scripture " here means every part of the Holy Scriptures mentioned in the preceding sentence. Indeed, γραφη has as definite a meaning in N.T. Greek as "Scripture" has in English, and is never used save of Holy Scripture. But I am bound in honesty to add that I believe the R.V. is wrong, albeit it has the authority of some of our earlier versions. The same construction occurs in eight other passages, viz., Rom. vii. 12 ; 1 Cor. xi. 30 ; 2 Cor. x. 10 ; 1 Tim. i. 15, ii. 3, iv. 4, 9 ; Heb. iv. 13. Why did the Revisers not read, *e.g*., " the holy commandment is also just and good" (Rom. vii. 12) ; and "many weak ones are also sickly " (1 Cor. xi. 30) ?

and in profanely applying these words to a romance of doubtful repute, Dr. Farrar denies inspiration altogether.

But "What is inspiration?" some one may demand. In another connection the inquiry might be apt; here it is the merest quibble. Plain men brush aside all the intricacies of the controversy which the answer involves, and seize upon the fact that the Bible is a divine revelation. But no one can yield to the spirit which pervades this book without coming to raise the question, "Have we a revelation at all?" The Higher Criticism, as a rationalistic crusade, has set itself to account for the Bible on natural principles; and this is the spirit which animates the Dean of Canterbury's treatise.

2

The Historical Errors of Daniel

" THE historical errors " of the Book of Daniel are the first ground of the critic's attack. Of these he enumerates the following :—

(1.) "There was no deportation in the third year of Jehoiakim."

(2.) "There was no King Belshazzar."

(3.) " There was no Darius the Mede."

(4.) " It is not true that there were only two Babylonian kings—there were five."

(5.) "Nor were there only four Persian kings—there were twelve."

(6.) Xerxes seems to be confounded with the last king of Persia.

(7.) And "All correct accounts of the reign of Antiochus Epiphanes seem to end about B.C. 164."

Such is the indictment under this head.

Two other points are included, but these have nothing to do with *history;* first, that the decrees of Nebuchadnezzar are extraordinary—which may at once be conceded; and secondly, that "the notion that a faithful Jew could become president of the Chaldean magi is impossible"—a statement which only exemplifies the thoughtless dogmatism of the writer, for, according to his own scheme, it was a *"holy and gifted Jew,"* brought up under the severe ritual of post-exilic days, who assigned this position to Daniel. A like remark applies to his criticism upon Dan. ii. 46—with this addition, that that criticism betokens either carelessness or malice on the part of the critics, for the passage in no way justifies the assertion that the prophet accepted either the worship or the sacrifice offered him.

So far as the other points are concerned, we may at once dismiss (4), (5), and (6), for the errors here ascribed to Daniel will be sought for in vain. They are "read into" the book by the perverseness or ignorance of the rationalists.[1]   And as for (7), where was the account of the reign of Antiochus to end, if not in the year of his death! The statement is one of numerous instances of slipshod carelessness in this extraordinary addition to our theological literature.

The Bible states that there was a deportation in the reign of Jehoiakim: the critic asserts there was none; and the Christian must decide between them.   Nothing can

---

[1] As regards (5) and (6), the way "kisses and kicks" alternate in Dr. Farrar's treatment of his mythical "Chasid" is amusing.   At one moment he is praised for his genius and erudition ; the next he is denounced as an ignoramus or a fool!   Considering how inseparably the history of Judah had been connected with the history of Persia, the suggestion that a cultured Jew of Maccabean days could have made the gross blunder here attributed to him is quite unworthy of notice.

And may I explain for the enlightenment of the critics that Dan. xi. 2 is a prophecy relating to the prophecy which precedes it ?   It is a consecutive prediction of events *within the period of the seventy weeks*.   There were to be "yet" (*i.e.*, after the rebuilding of Jerusalem) "three kings in Persia."   These were Darius Nothus, Artaxerxes Mnemon, and Ochus ; the brief and merely nominal reigns of Xerxes II., Sogdianus, and Arogus being ignored—two of them, indeed, being omitted from the canon of Ptolemy.   "The fourth" (and last) king was Darius Codomanus, whose fabulous wealth attracted the cupidity of the Greeks.

be clearer than the language of Chronicles;[1] and, even regarding the book as a purely secular record, it is simply preposterous to reject without a shadow of reason the chronicler's statement on a matter of such immense interest and importance in the national history. But, it is objected, Kings and Jeremiah are silent upon the subject. If this were true, which it is not, it would be an additional reason for turning to Chronicles to supply the omission. But Kings gives clear corroboration of Chronicles. Speaking of Jehoiakim, it says: "In his days Nebuchadnezzar, King of Babylon, came up, and Jehoiakim became his servant three years; then he turned and rebelled against him."[2] Daniel[3] tells us this was in his *third* year, and that Jerusalem was besieged upon the occasion. This difficulty again springs from the habit of "reading into" Scripture more than it says. There is not a word about a taking by storm. The king was a mere puppet, and presum-

---

[1] 2 Chron. xxxvi. 6.   [2] 2 Kings xxiv. 1.   [3] Ch. i. 1.

ably he made his submission as soon as the
city was invested. Nebuchadnezzar took him
prisoner, but afterwards relented, and left him
in Jerusalem as his vassal, a position he had
till then held under the King of Egypt.

But Dr. Farrar's statements here are
worthy of fuller notice, so thoroughly typical are they of his style and methods. For
three years Jehoiakim was Nebuchadnezzar's
vassal. This is admitted, and Scripture
accounts for it by recording a Babylonian
invasion in his third year. But, says the
critic :—

"It was not till the following year, when Nebuchadrezzar, acting as his father's general, had
defeated Egypt at the battle of Carchemish, that
any siege of Jerusalem would have been possible. Nor did Nebuchadrezzar advance against
the Holy City even after the battle of Carchemish,
but dashed home across the desert to secure the
crown of Babylon on hearing the news of his father's
death."

The idea of dashing across the desert
from Carchemish to Babylon is worthy of
a board-school essay! The critic is here
adopting the record of the Babylonian

historian Berosus, in complete unconscious-
ness of the significance of his testimony.
We learn from Berosus that it was as Prince-
royal of Babylon, at the head of his father's
army, that Nebuchadnezzar invaded Palestine.
And, after recording how in the course of
that expedition Nebuchadnezzar heard of
his father's death, the historian goes on to
relate that he " committed *the captives he
had taken from the Jews* " to the charge
of others, " while he went in haste over the
desert to Babylon." [1] Could corroboration of
Scripture be more complete and emphatic?
The fact that he had Jewish captives is
evidence that he had invaded Judea. Proof
of it is afforded by the further fact that
the desert lay between him and Babylon.
Carchemish was in the far north by the
Euphrates, and the road thence to the
Chaldean capital lay clear of the desert
altogether. Moreover, the battle of Carchemish was fought in Jehoiakim's *fourth*
year, and therefore after Nebuchadnezzar's
accession, whereas the invasion of Judea was

---

[1] Josephus, *Contra Apion*, i. 19.

during Nabopolassar's lifetime, and therefore
in Jehoiakim's *third* year, precisely as the
Book of Daniel avers.[1]

It only remains to add that Scripture nowhere speaks of a *general* " deportation " in
the third year of Jehoiakim.   Here, as elsewhere, the critic attributes his own errors
to the Bible, and then proceeds to refute
them.   The narrative is explicit that on
this occasion Nebuchadnezzar returned with
no captives save a few cadets of the royal
house and of the noble families.   But Dr.
Farrar writes : " *Among the captives* were
certain of the king's seed and of the princes."
Nor is this all : he goes on to say, " They
are called ' children,' and the word, together
with the context, seems to imply that they
were boys of the age of from twelve to fourteen."   What Daniel says is that these, *the
only captives*, were " skilful in all wisdom, and

---

[1] The question of course arises how this battle should
have been fought *after* the successful campaign of the preceding year.   There are reasonable explanations of this, but
I offer none.   Scripture has suffered grievously from the
eagerness of its defenders to put forward hypotheses to
explain seeming difficulties.

cunning in knowledge, and understanding science." What prodigies those Jewish boys must have been! The word translated "children" in the A.V. is more correctly rendered "youths" in the R.V. Its scope may be inferred from the use of it in 1 Kings xii. 8, which tells us that Rehoboam "forsook the counsel of the old men, and took counsel with the *young men* that were grown up with him." This last point is material mainly as showing the animus of the critic.[1]

But the Scripture speaks of *King* Nebuchadnezzar in the third year of Jehoiakim, whereas it was not till his fourth year that Nabopolassar died. No doubt. And a writer of Maccabean days, with the history of Berosus before him, would probably have

---

[1] The only reason for representing Daniel as a mere boy of twelve or fourteen is that thereby discredit is cast upon the statement that three years later he was placed at the head of "the wise men" of Babylon. It is with a real sense of distress and pain that I find myself compelled to use such language. But it would need a volume to expose the errors, misstatements, and perversions of which the above are typical instances. They occur in every chapter of Dr. Farrar's book.

noticed the point.   But the so-called in-accuracy is precisely one of the incidental proofs that the Book of Daniel was the work of a contemporary of Nebuchadnezzar. The historian of the future will never assert that Queen Victoria lived at one time in Kensington Palace, though the statement will be found in the newspapers which recorded the unveiling of her statue in Kensington Gardens.

The references to Jeremiah raise the question whether the book records the utterances of an inspired prophet, or whether, as Dr. Farrar's criticisms assume, the author of the book wrote merely as a religious teacher.[1] This question, however, is too large to treat of here ; and the discussion of it is wholly un-necessary, for the careful student will find in Jeremiah the clearest proof that Scripture is right and the critics wrong.   The objection

---

[1] The careful reader of Dr. Farrar's book will not fail to see that his references to the Scriptures generally imply that the prophecies came by the will of the prophets ; whereas Holy Scripture declares that "No prophecy ever came by the will of man ; but men spake from God, being moved by the Holy Ghost" (2 Pet. i. 20, 21).

depends on confounding the seventy years of the "Servitude to Babylon" with the seventy years of "the Desolations of Jerusalem"—another of the numerous blunders which discredit the work under review.[1] "The Captivity," which is confounded with both, was not an era of seventy years at all.

The prophecy of the twenty-fifth chapter of Jeremiah was a warning addressed to the people who remained in the land after the servitude had begun, that if they continued impenitent and rebellious, God would bring upon them a further judgment—the terrible scourge of "the Desolations." The prophecy of the twenty-ninth chapter was a message of hope to the Jews of the Captivity. And what was that message? That "after seventy years be accomplished for Babylon, I will visit you, and perform my good word toward you, in causing you to return to this place."[2] And that promise was faithfully

---

[1] P. 289.

[2] Jer. xxix. 10, R.V. The word is *for* (not *at*) Babylon. These "seventy years" dated, not from their deportation to Babylonia as captives, but from their subjection to the suzerainty of Babylon.

fulfilled. The Servitude began in the third
year of Jehoiakim, B.C. 606.[1] It ended in
B.C. 536, when Cyrus issued his decree for
the return of the exiles. By the test of
chronology, therefore — the severest test
which can be applied to historical statements — the absolute accuracy of these
Scriptures is established.[2]

---

[1] That is, the year beginning with Nisan, B.C. 606, and
ending with Adar, B.C. 605.

[2] Owing to the importance of this Jehoiakim "error" I
have added an *excursus* upon the subject. See Appendix I.
p. 153, *post.*

3

Historical Errors Continued:
Belshazzar and Darius the Mede

PROFESSOR Driver acknowledges "the possibility that Nabunahid may have sought to strengthen his position by marrying a daughter of Nebuchadnezzar, in which case the latter might be spoken of as Belshazzar's father (= grandfather, by Hebrew usage)."[1] And the author of the *Ancient Monarchies*, our best historical authority here, tells us that Nabonidus (Nabunahid) "had associated with him in the government his son Belshazzar or Bel-shar-uzur, the grandson of the great Nebuchadnezzar," and "in his father's absence Belshazzar took the direction of affairs within the city."[2] The only question, therefore, is whether Belshazzar, being thus left as regent at Babylon when his father was

---

[1] *Book of Daniel*, p. li.
[2] Rawlinson's *Ancient Monarchies*, vol. iii. p. 70.

absent at Borsippa in command of the army, would be addressed as *king*. But Dr. Farrar settles the matter by asserting that "there was no King Belshazzar," and that Belshazzar was "conquered in Borsippa."[1] This last statement is a mere blunder.

The accuracy of Daniel in this matter is confirmed in a manner which is all the more striking because it is wholly incidental. Why did Belshazzar purpose to make Daniel the *third* ruler in the kingdom? The natural explanation is, that he himself was but *second*.

"Unhappily for their very precarious hypothesis," Dr. Farrar remarks, "the translation 'third ruler' appears to be *entirely untenable*. It means 'one of a board of three.'"[2] As a test of the author's erudition and candour this deserves particular notice. Every scholar, of course, is aware that there is not a word about a "board of three" in the text. This is exegesis, not translation. But is it correct exegesis?

Under the Persian rule there was a cabinet

---

[1] P. 54.   [2] P. 57.

of three, as the sixth chapter tells us; but
there is no authority whatever for supposing
such a body existed under the empire which
it supplanted.   As regards chapter v., it will
satisfy most people to know that the rendering which Dr. Farrar declares to be "entirely
untenable" has been adopted by the Old Testament company of Revisers.   And I have
been at the pains to ascertain that the passage was carefully considered, that they had
no difficulty in deciding in favour of the reading of the A.V., and that it was not until
their final revision that the alternative rendering "one of three" was admitted into the
margin.   In the distinguished Professor
Kautzsch's recent work on the Old Testament,[1] representing the latest and best German scholarship, he adheres to the rendering
"third ruler in the kingdom," and his note is,
"either as one of three over the whole kingdom, or as third by the side of the king and
the king's mother."   Behrmann, too, in his
recent commentary, adopts the same reading —"as third he was to have authority

---

[1] *Die Heilige Schrift des Alten Testaments.*

in the kingdom," and adds a note referring to the king and his mother as first and second.[1]

This surely will suffice to silence the critic's objection, and to cast suspicion upon his fairness as a controversialist.[2]

But, we are told, the archæological discoveries of the last few years dispose of the whole question, and compel us entirely to

---

[1] In reply to an inquiry I addressed to him, the Chief Rabbi wrote to me as follows : " I have carefully considered the question you laid before me at our pleasant meeting on Sunday relative to the correct interpretation of the passages in Daniel, chapter v., verses 7 and 16.   I cannot absolutely find fault with Archdeacon Farrar for translating the words 'the third part of the kingdom,' as he follows herein two of our Hebrew commentators of great repute, Rashi and Ibn Ezra.   On the other hand, others of our commentators, such as Saadia, Jachja, &c., translate this passage as 'he shall be the third ruler in the kingdom.'   This rendering seems to be more strictly in accord with the literal meaning of the words as shown by Dr. Winer in his *Grammatik des Chaldaismus*.   It also receives confirmation from Sir Henry Rawlinson's remarkable discovery, according to which Belshazzar was the eldest son of King Nabonidus, and associated with him in the government, so that the person next in honour would be the third."

[2] This applies equally to Prof. Driver's note, which says "The rendering of A.V. is certainly untenable."   And his reference to the LXX. is unfair, seeing that his view is refuted by the version of Theodotion, which is of higher authority than that to which he appeals.

reconstruct the traditional history of the Persian conquest of Babylon. "We now possess the actual records of Nabonidos and Cyrus," Professor Sayce tells us, and he adds, "They are records the truth of which cannot be doubted."[1] What "simple child-like faith" these good men have in ancient records, Holy Scripture only excepted! The principal record here in question is "the Annalistic tablet of Cyrus," an inscription of which the transparent design is to represent his conquest of Babylon as the fulfilment of a divine mission, and the realisation of the wishes of the conquered. And any document of the kind, whether dated in the sixth century B.C. or the nineteenth century A.D., is open to grave suspicion, and should be received with caution. Even kings may pervert the truth, and State-papers may falsify facts! But even assuming its accuracy, it in no way supports the conclusions which are based upon it. No advance will be made towards a solution of these ques-

---

[1] *The Higher Criticism and the Verdict of the Monuments*, p. 498.

tions until our Christian scholars shake
themselves free from the baneful influence
of the sceptics, whose blind hostility to Holy
Scripture unfits them for dealing with any
controversy of the kind. The following is
a typical instance of the effect of the influence I deprecate :—

"But Belshazzar never became king in his
father's place. No mention is made of him at
the end of the Annalistic tablet, and it would
therefore appear that he was no longer in command of the Babylonian army when the invasion
of Cyrus took place. Owing to the unfortunate
lacuna in the middle of the tablet we have no
account of what became of him, but since we are
told not only of the fate of Nabonidos, but also
of the death of his wife, it seems probable that
Belshazzar was dead. At any rate, when Cyrus
entered Babylonia he had already disappeared
from history. Here, then, the account given by
the Book of Daniel is at variance with the testimony of the inscriptions. But the contradictions
do not end here. The Biblical story implies that
Babylon was taken by storm; at all events it expressly states that 'the king of the Chaldeans was
slain.' Nabonidos, the Babylonian king, however,
was not slain, and Cyrus entered Babylon 'in
peace.' Nor was Belshazzar the son of Nebuchad-

rezzar, as we are repeatedly told in the fifth chapter of Daniel."[1]

May I criticise the critic? Daniel nowhere avers that Belshazzar became king in his father's place. On the contrary, it clearly implies that he reigned as his father's viceroy. Daniel nowhere suggests that he was in command of the Babylonian army. The Annalistic tablet, on the other hand, tells us that *Nabonidus* was at the head of the army, and that he was at Sippara when the Persian invasion took place, and fled when that town

---

[1] *The Higher Criticism and the Verdict of the Monuments*, pp. 525, 526. This last point is typical of the inaccuracy and pertinacity of the critics. We are nowhere told in Daniel that Belshazzar was the son of Nebuchadnezzar. We are told that *he was so addressed* at the Court of Babylon, which is a wholly different matter. He was probably a descendant of the great king, but it is certain that if, rightly or wrongly, he claimed relationship with him, no one at his court would dispute the claim. In a table of Babylonian kings I find mention of a daughter of Nebuchadnezzar who married the father of Nabonidus (*Trans. Vict. Inst.*, vol. xviii. p. 99). This of course would dispose of the whole difficulty. She, perhaps, was "the king's mother," whose death eight years before was followed by national mourning (*Annal. Tablet*). To trade on the word "son" is a mere quibble *ad captandum vulgus*, which has been exposed again and again. (See Pusey's *Daniel*, p. 405, and Rawlinson's *Egypt and Babylon*, p. 155.)

opened its gates to the invaders. To the fact that more than half of the inscription is lost Professor Sayce attributes the absence of all mention of Belshazzar. And yet he goes on to assume, without a shadow of evidence, that he had died before the date of the expedition; and upon this utterly baseless conjecture he founds the equally baseless assertion that "Daniel is at variance with the testimony of the inscriptions"! As a matter of fact, however, the tablet is not silent about Belshazzar. On the contrary, it expressly refers to him, and records his death.

But to resume. Daniel nowhere avers that "Babylon was taken by storm." Neither is it said, "the king of the Chaldeans was slain"; the words are explicit that "*Belshazzar*, the Chaldean king, was slain." How his death was brought about we are not told. He may have fallen in repelling an assault upon the palace, or his death may have been caused in furtherance of the priestly conspiracy in favour of Cyrus, or the "wise men" may have compassed it in revenge for the preferment of Daniel.

All this is mere conjecture. Scripture merely tells us that he was slain, and that Darius the Mede, aged about sixty-two, "*received* the kingdom." The same word occurs again in ii. 6 ("Ye shall *receive* of me gifts," &c.), and in vii. 18 ("The saints of the Most High shall *receive* the kingdom "). No word could more fitly describe the enthronement of a vassal king or viceroy. No language could be more apt to record a peaceful change of dynasty, such as, according to some of the students of the inscriptions, took place when Nabonidus lost the throne.

But this is not all; and the sequel may well excite the reader's astonishment. First, we are asked to draw inferences from the silence of this document, though we possess but mutilated fragments of it, and, for ought we know, the lost portions may have contained matter to refute these very inferences. And secondly, accepting the contents of the fragments which remain, the allegation that they contradict the Book of Daniel has no better foundation than Professor Sayce's

heretical reading of them ; and if we appeal
to a more trustworthy guide, we shall find
that, so far from being inconsistent with the
sacred narrative, they afford the most striking
confirmation of its truth.

According to this tablet, "Sippara was
taken without fighting, and Nabonidus fled."
This was on the 14th day of Tammuz ;[1]
and on the 16th, "Gobryas and the soldiers
of Cyrus entered Babylon without fighting."
On the 3rd day of Marchesvan, that is, four
months later,[2] Cyrus himself arrived. Following this comes the significant statement :
"The 11th day of Marchesvan, during the
night, Gobryas was on the bank of the river.
The son of the king died"; or, as Professor
Driver reads it, "Gubaru *made an assault,
and slew the king's son.*"[3]   Then follows the
mention of the national mourning and of
the State burial conducted by Cambyses,
the son of Cyrus, in person. But instead of
"the *son* of the king," Professor Sayce here
reads "the *wife* of the king," and upon this

---

[1] June—July.   [2] October—November.
[3] See p. 36, *post.*

error rests the entire superstructure of his attack upon the accuracy of Daniel.[1]

Nor is this all. The main statements in the tablet may reasonably be accepted. We may assume that the Persian troops entered Sippara on the 14th Tammuz, and reached Babylon on the 16th. But the assertion that in both cases the entry was peaceful will, of course, be received with reserve. Professor Sayce, however, would have us believe it all implicitly, and he goes on to assert that Cyrus was King of Babylon from the 14th Tammuz, and therefore that Daniel's mention of the death of Belshazzar and the accession of Darius the Mede is purely mythical. He dismisses to a footnote the awkward fact that we have commercial tablets dated in the reign of Nabonidus throughout the year, and even after the arrival of Cyrus himself; and his gloss upon this fact is that it gives further proof that the change of dynasty was a peaceful one! It gives proof clear and conclusive that during this period Nabonidus was still recog-

---

[1] See Appendix II., p. 160, *post.*

nised as king, and therefore that Cyrus was not yet master of the city. As a matter of fact we have not a single "Cyrus" tablet in this year dated from Babylon. All, with one exception, the source of which is not known, were made in Sippara.[1]

But who was this personage whose death was the occasion of a great national mourning and a State funeral? As the context shows clearly that "the king" referred to was not Cyrus, he can have been no other than Nabonidus; and as "the king's son," so frequently mentioned in the earlier fragments of the inscription and in the contract tablets, is admittedly Belshazzar,[2] there is no reason whatever to doubt that it was he whose death and obsequies are here recorded.

What then does all this lead us to? The careful and impartial historian, repudiating the iconoclastic zeal of the controversialist, will set himself to consider how these facts can be harmonised with other records sacred

---

[1] See p. 164, *post.*   [2] Sayce, p. 525.

and profane ; and the task will not prove a difficult one. Accepting the fact that at the time of the Persian invasion Nabonidus was absent from Babylon, he will be prepared to find that "the king's son" held command in the capital as viceroy. Accepting the fact that the Persian army entered Babylon in the month Tammuz, and that Cyrus arrived four months later, but yet that Nabonidus was still recognised as king, he will explain the seeming paradox by inferring that the invaders were in possession only of a part of the vast city of Nebuchadnezzar, and that Belshazzar, surrounded by his court and the wealthy classes of the community, still refused to yield. Accepting the fact that Cyrus desired to represent his conquest as a bloodless one, he will be prepared to assume that force was resorted to only after a long delay and when diplomacy was exhausted. And he will not be surprised to find that when at last, either in an attack upon the palace, or by some act of treachery in furtherance of the cause of the invaders, " Belshazzar the Chaldean king was slain," the fact was veiled by the euphemistic announcement that "the king's son died." [1]

But while the record is thus shown to be entirely consistent with Daniel, so far as the mention of Belshazzar is concerned, what room does it leave for Darius the Mede? The answer is that the inscription fails us at this precise point. "The rest of the text is destroyed, but the fragments of it which remain indicate that it described the various attempts made by Cyrus and his son Kambyses, after the overthrow of Nabonidus, to settle the affairs of Babylonia and conciliate the priesthood." Such is Professor Sayce's own testimony.[2] In a word, it is

---

[1] When the fall of the Empire scattered the Secret Service staff of the French Prefecture of Police, many strange things came to my knowledge. I then learned that Count D'Orsay's death was caused by a pistol-bullet aimed at the Emperor, with whom he was walking arm-in-arm. But it was publicly announced, and universally believed, that he died of a carbuncle in the back. If, even in these days of newspapers, facts can be thus disguised for reasons of State, who will pretend that the circumstances of Belshazzar's death may not have been thus concealed in Chaldea twenty-five centuries ago? Moreover, Professor Driver's reading of the tablet (see p. 32, *ante*) renders even this suggestion unnecessary.

[2] P. 503.

doubtful whether the tablet mentions Darius or not, but it is certain that any such mention would be purely incidental, and wholly outside the purpose with which the inscription was framed. While its mention of him, therefore, would be conclusive, its silence respecting him would prove nothing.

Nor will the omission of his name from the commercial tablets decide the matter either way. If, as Daniel indicates, Darius was but a viceroy or vassal king, his suzerain's name would, in the ordinary course, be used for this purpose, just as the name of Nabonidus was used during the regency of Belshazzar.

But who was this Darius? Various hypotheses are maintained by scholars of eminence. By some he is identified with Gobryas, and this suggestion commends itself on many grounds.[1] Others, again, fol-

---

[1] See Appendix II., *post.* The language of the Cyrus inscription is very striking, as indicating that Gobryas was no mere subordinate ; *e.g.,* "Peace to the city did Cyrus establish. Peace to all the princes of Babylon did Gobryas his governor proclaim. Governors in Babylon he (Gobryas) appointed."

low the view adopted by Josephus, according to which Darius was "the son and successor of Astyages"—namely, Cyaxares II. Xenophon is the only authority for the existence of such a king, but his testimony has been rejected too lightly on the plea that his *Cyropædia* is but a romance. The writers of historical romances, however, do not invent kings. Yet another suggestion remains, that Darius was the personal name of "Astyages," the last king of the Medes. "This," says Bishop Westcott, "appears to satisfy all the conditions of the problem."[1]

Although I myself adopt the first of these rival hypotheses, my task is merely to show that the question is still open, and that the grounds on which it is now sought to prove it closed are such as would satisfy no one who is competent to form an opinion upon the evidence. Though Professor Driver here remarks that "there seems to be no room for such a ruler," he is careful to add

---

[1] Smith's *Bible Dictionary*, 1st ed., article "Darius." Dr. Westcott adds : "The name Astyages was national and not personal, and Ahasuerus represents the name Cyaxares borne by the father of Astyages."

that the circumstances are not inconsistent with either his existence or his office, "and a cautious criticism will not build too much on the silence of the inscriptions, where many certainly remain yet to be brought to light." [1]

The identity of Darius the Mede is one of the most interesting problems in the Daniel controversy, and it is a problem which cannot be ignored. The critics do not dispose of it by declaring the Book of Daniel to be a "pseud-epigraph" of Maccabean days. Accepting that hypothesis for the sake of argument, the mention of Darius remains to be accounted for. Some writers reject it as "pure fiction"; others denounce it as a "sheer blunder." Though these are wholly inconsistent hypotheses, Dr. Farrar, *more suo*, adopts both. Both, however, are alike untenable; and the "*avowed* fiction" theory may be dismissed as unworthy of notice. The writer would have had no possible motive for inventing a "Darius," for the

---

[1] The *Introduction*, &c., p. 469. In the *Addenda* note to 3rd ed., Professor Driver seeks to qualify this, misled by Professor Sayce's argument. But see pp. 33, 34, *ante*.

events of Daniel vi. might just as well have
been assigned to some other reign, and a
figment of the kind would have marred his
book.   The suggestion is preposterous.

And *ex hypothesi*, the author must have
been a man of extraordinary genius and of
great erudition.   He would have had before
him historical records now lost, such as the
history of Berosus.   He would have had
access to the authorities upon which the
book of the *Antiquities* is based; for the
student of Josephus cannot fail to see that
his history is partly derived from sources
other than the Book of Daniel.   And be-
sides all this, he would have had the Book
of Ezra, which records how Darius the
Persian issued an edict to give effect to the
decree of Cyrus for the rebuilding of the
Temple, and also the prophecies of Haggai
and Zechariah, which bring this fact into
still greater prominence.   It may safely be
averred, therefore, that no intelligent schoolboy, no devout peasant, in all Judah could
have been guilty of a blunder so gross and
stupid as that which is attributed to this

"holy and gifted Jew," the author of the most famous and successful literary fraud the world has ever seen! The "sheer blunder" theory may be rejected as sheer nonsense.

Accepting, then, for the sake of argument, the pseud-epigraph theory of Daniel, the book gives proof of a definite and well-established historical tradition that when Cyrus conquered Babylon, "Darius the Mede received the kingdom." How, then, is that tradition to be accounted for? The question demands an answer, but the critics have none to offer.

4

"Philological Peculiarities": The Language of Daniel

"THE philological peculiarities of the book" constitute the next ground of the critic's attack on Daniel. "The Hebrew" (he declares) "is pronounced by the majority of experts to be of a later character than the time assumed for it." The Aramaic also is marked by idioms of a later period, familiar to the Palestinian Jews.[1] And not only are Persian words employed in the book, but it contains certain Greek words, which, it is said, could not have been in use in Babylon during the exile.

---

[1] The opening passage of Daniel, from ch. i. 1 to ch. ii. 3, is written in the sacred Hebrew, and this is resumed at ch. viii. 1 and continued to the end. The intervening portion, from ch. ii. 4 to the end of ch. vii., is written in Chaldee or Aramaic. Professor Cheyne accepts a suggestion of Lenormant's that the whole book was written in Hebrew, but that the original of ii. 14 to vii. was lost (Smith's *Bible Dict.*, art. "Daniel").

Here is Professor Driver's summary of the argument under this head :—

"The verdict of the language of Daniel is thus clear. The *Persian* words presuppose a period after the Persian Empire had been well established : the Greek words *demand*, the Hebrew *supports*, and the Aramaic *permits*, a date after the conquest of Palestine by Alexander the Great (B.C. 332). With our present knowledge, this is as much as the language authorises us definitely to affirm." [1]

Now, the strength of this case depends on one point. Any number of argumentative presumptions may be rebutted by opposing evidence ; but here, it is alleged, we have proof which admits of no answer : the Greek words in Daniel *demand* a date which destroys the genuineness of the book. Will the reader believe it that the only foundation for this is the presence of *two* words which are alleged to be Greek ! Dr. Farrar insists on three, but one of these (*kitharos*) is practically given up.[2]

---

[1] *The Introduction*, p. 476, and *The Book of Daniel*, p. lxiii.

[2] In Bertholdt's day the critics counted *ten* Greek words in Daniel : they have now come down to *two*. Dr. Pusey denies that there are any.

The story was lately told that at a church bazaar in Lincoln, held under episcopal patronage, the alarm was given that a thief was at work, and two of the visitors had lost their purses.   In the excitement which followed, the stolen purses, emptied of course of their contents, were found in the bishop's pocket.   The Higher Criticism would have handed him over to the police!   Do the critics understand the very rudiments of the science of weighing evidence?   The presence of the stolen purses did not "demand" the conviction of the bishop.   Neither should the presence of the Greek words decide the fate of Daniel.   There was no doubt, moreover, as to the identity of the purses, while Dr. Pusey and others dispute the derivation of the words.   But in the one case as in the other the question would remain, How did they come to be where they were found?

The Talmud declares that, in common with some other parts of the canon, Daniel was edited by the men of the Great Synagogue—a college which is supposed to have been founded by Nehemiah, and which con-

tinued until it gave place to the Great Sanhedrim. May not this be the explanation of
all these philological difficulties? This is not
to have recourse to a baseless conjecture in
order to evade well-founded objections: it is
merely to give due weight to an authori-
tative tradition, the very existence of which
is *prima facie* proof of its truth.[1]

It may be added that in view of recent
discoveries no competent scholar would

---

[1] The attempt to explain in this way difficulties of another
kind is to force the hypothesis unduly. But assuming, what
there is no reason whatever to doubt, that such a revision
took place, we should expect to find that familiar idioms
would be substituted for others that were deemed archaic,
that familiar words would be substituted for terms which
then seemed strange or uncouth to the Jews of Palestine,
and that names like Nebuchadrezzar would be altered to
suit the then received orthography. And the "immense ana-
chronism," if such it were, of using the word "Chaldeans"
as synonymous with the caste of wise men is thus simply
and fully explained.

As regards the name Nebuchadnezzar, it is hard to re-
press a feeling of indignation against the dishonesty of the
critics. They plainly imply that this spelling is peculiar to
Daniel. The fact is that the name occurs in nine of the
books of the Old Testament, and in all of them, with the
single exception of Ezekiel, it appears in this form. In
Jeremiah it is spelt in both ways, proving clearly that the
now received orthography was in use when the Book of
Daniel was written, or else that the spelling of the name
throughout the sacred books is entirely a matter of editing.

now reproduce without reserve the argument based on the presence of foreign words in the book. The fact is, the evolution theory has thrown its shadow across this controversy. The extraordinary conceit which marks our much-vaunted age has hitherto led us to assume that, in what has been regarded as a prehistoric period, men were slowly emerging from barbarism, that written records were wanting, and that there was no interchange among nations in the sphere either of scholarship or of trade. It is now known, however, that at even a far earlier period the nations bordering upon the Mediterranean possessed a literature and enjoyed a civilisation of no mean excellence. Merchants and philosophers travelled freely from land to land,[1] carrying with them their

---

[1] May not all that is truest and best in Buddhism be thus traced to the great prophet-prince of the exile? Gautama was a contemporary of Daniel. And when he set out upon his long pilgrimage in search of truth and light, may he not have found his way to Babylon, then the most famous centre both of civilisation and of religion. And visiting the broad-walled city, he could not fail to come under the influence of Daniel. Daniel was born about B.C. 624; and, according to Sir E. Arnold (*Light of Asia*, Preface), Gautama was born about B.C. 620.

wares and their learning; and to appeal to
the Greek words in Daniel as proof that the
book was written after the date of Alexander's conquests, no longer savours of
scholarship. According to Professor Sayce,
"there were Greek colonies on the coast of
Palestine in the time of Hezekiah"—a century before Daniel was born; "and they
already enjoyed so much power there that a
Greek usurper was made King of Ashdod.
The Tel el-Amarna tablets have enabled
us to carry back a contract between Greece
and Canaan to a still earlier period."[1] Indeed he goes on to indicate the possibility
"that there was intercourse and contact between the Canaanites or Hebrews in Palestine and the Greeks of the Ægean as far
back as the age of Moses."

But this is not all. Will the reader
believe it, I ask again with increasing
emphasis and indignation, that the Greek
words, the presence of which is held to
"demand" the rejection of the Book of
Daniel, are merely the names of musical

---

[1] *The Higher Criticism and the Monuments*, pp. 494, 495.

instruments? If the instruments themselves came from Greece it might be assumed that they would carry with them to Babylon the names by which they were known in the land of their origin. In no other sphere would men listen to what passes for proof when Scripture is assailed. In no other sphere would such trifling be tolerated. What would be thought of a tribunal which convicted a notorious thief of petty larceny on such evidence as this?

The Persian words are of still less account. That the Persian language was unknown among the cultured classes in Babylon is incredible. That it was widely known is suggested by the ease with which the Persian rule was accepted. The position which Daniel attained under that rule renders it probable in the extreme that he himself was a Persian scholar. And the date of his closing vision makes it certain that his book was compiled after that rule was established.

But, it will be answered, the philological argument does not rest upon points like these ; its strength lies in the general character of the language in which the book is written. The question here raised, as Dr. Farrar justly says, "involves delicate problems on which an independent and a valuable opinion can only be offered" by scholars of a certain class and very few in number.[1]

But the student will find that their decision is by no means unanimous or clear. And of course their *dicta* must be considered in connection with evidence of other kinds which it is beyond their province to deal with. Dr. Pusey's magnificent work, in which the whole subject is handled with the greatest erudition and care, is not dismissed by others with the contempt which Dr. Farrar evinces for a man who is fired by the enthusiasm of faith in the Bible. In his judgment the Hebrew of Daniel is "just what one should expect at the age at which he lived."[2]

---

[1] Dr. Farrar's words are, "by the merest handful of living scholars" (p. 17). How many scholars make a "handful" he does not tell us, and of the two he proceeds to appeal to, one is not living but dead !

[2] Pusey, p. 578.

And one of the highest living authorities, who has been quoted in this controversy as favouring a late date for the Book of Daniel, writes in reply to an inquiry I have addressed to him : " I am now of opinion that it is a very difficult task to settle the age of any portion of that book from its language." This is also the opinion of Professor Cheyne, a thoroughly hostile witness. His words are : " From the Hebrew of the Book of Daniel no important inference as to its date can be safely drawn." [1]

And, lastly, appeal may be made to Dr. Farrar himself, who remarks with signal fairness, but with strange inconsistency, that " Perhaps nothing certain can be inferred from the philological examination either of the Hebrew or of the Chaldee portions of the book." [2] And again, still more definitely, he declares : " The character of the language proves nothing." [3] This testimony, carrying as it does the exceptional weight which attaches to the admissions of a prejudiced

[1] *Ency. Brit.*, art. "Daniel," p. 804.
[2] P. 17.   [3] P. 89.

and hostile witness, might be accepted as decisive of the whole question. And the fact being what is here stated, the stress laid on grounds thus admitted to be faulty and inconclusive is proof only of a determination by fair means or foul to discredit the Book of Daniel.

In his *History of the Criminal Law*, Sir James Fitzjames Stephen declares that, as no kind of evidence more demands the test of cross-examination than that of experts, their proper place is the witness chair and not the judgment seat. Therefore when Professor Driver announces "the *verdict* of the language of Daniel," he goes entirely outside his proper province. The opinions of the philologist are entitled to the highest respect, but the "verdict" rests with those who have practical acquaintance with the science of evidence.

Before turning away from this part of the subject, it may be well to appeal to yet another witness, and he shall be one whose competency Dr. Farrar acknowledges, and none will question. His words, more-

over, have an interest and value far beyond
the present controversy, and deserve most
careful consideration by all who have been
stumbled or misled by the arrogant dogmatism of the so-called Higher Critics.   The
following quotation is from *An Essay on the
Place of Ecclesiasticus in Semitic Literature*
by Professor Margoliouth : [1]—

"My lamented colleague, Dr. Edersheim, and I,
misled by the very late date assigned by eminent
scholars to the books of the Bible, had worked
under the tacit assumption that the language of
Ben - Sira was the language of the Prophets ;
whereas in reality he wrote the language of the
Rabbis " (p. 6).

It should be explained that the Proverbs
of Jesus the son of Sirach have come down
to us in a Greek translation, but the
character of that translation is such that the
reconstruction of the original Hebrew text
is a task within the capacity of competent
scholarship, and a preface to that translation
fixes the date of the book as not later than
about B.C. 200.   But to resume :—

---

[1] Clarendon Press, 1890.

" If by 200 B.C. the whole Rabbinic farrago, with its terms and phrases and idioms and particles, was developed, . . . then between Ben-Sira and the Books of the Old Testament there must lie centuries—nay, there must lie, in most cases, the deep waters of the Captivity, the grave of the old-Hebrew and the old Israel, and the womb of the new-Hebrew and the new Israel. If Hebrew, like any other language, has a history, then Isaiah (first or second) must be separated from Ecclesiastes by a gulf; but a yet greater gulf must yawn between Ecclesiastes and Ecclesiaticus, for in the interval a whole dictionary has been invented of philosophical terms such as we traced above, of logical phrases, . . . legal expressions, . . . nor have the structure and grammar of the language experienced less serious alteration. . . . It may be, if ever Ben-Sira is properly restored, . . . that while some students are engaged in bringing down the date of every chapter in the Bible so late as to leave no room for prophecy and revelation, others will endeavour to find out how early the professedly post-exilian books can be put back, so as to account for the divergence between their awkward middle-Hebrew and the rich and eloquent new-Hebrew of Ben-Sira. However this may be, hypotheses which place any portion of the classical or old-Hebrew Scriptures between the middle-Hebrew of Nehemiah and the new-Hebrew of Ben-Sira will surely require some reconsideration, or at least have to be harmonised in some way with the history of the language, before they can be unconditionally accepted."

These weighty words have received striking confirmation by the recent discovery of the " Cairene Ecclesiasticus," a Hebrew MS. the genuineness of which is maintained by most of the critics, though others regard it as merely an attempt to reconstruct the original of Ben-Sira.   According to Dr. Schechter, who has edited the document for the University of Cambridge, an examination of the language establishes "the conclusion that at the period in which B.-S. composed his 'Wisdom' classical Hebrew was already a thing of the past, the real language of the period being that Hebrew idiom which we know from the Mishnah and cognate Rabbinic literature."   And again, after freely quoting from Ben-Sira : "These specimens are enough to show that in the times of B.-S. the new-Hebrew dialect had long advanced beyond the transitory stage known to us from the later Biblical books, and had already reached, both in respect of grammar and of phraseology, that degree of development to which the Mishnah bears testimony." [1]

---

[1] *The Wisdom of Ben-Sira, &c.*, by S. Schechter, M.A., Litt.D., &c., and C. Taylor, D.D., Master of St. John's College, Cambridge (Cambridge University Press, 1899). As Professor Driver and his school have unreservedly accepted this MS., it is not open to them to plead that its genuineness is doubtful. And if Professor Margoliouth's judgment should ultimately prevail that it is a forgery of late date—the tenth or eleventh century — it would be still, as an attempt to reconstruct the Hebrew original, a notable confirmation of the views and opinions above cited.

5

The Positive Evidence
in Favor of Daniel

THE critics claim a competency to judge whether this portion or that of the canon of Scripture be divinely inspired, and in the exercise of this faculty they have decided that certain passages of Daniel give proof that the book could not have a divine sanction. Their *dicta* on this subject will have weight with us just in proportion to our ignorance of Scripture. The opening chapters of the book which follows Daniel in the canon present far greater difficulties in this respect, and yet the prophetic character of Hosea is unquestionable. Other Scriptures also might be cited to point the same moral; but as these pretensions of the critics are not accepted by Christians generally, the matter need not be further discussed.

Still more summarily we may dismiss

Dean Farrar's argument from the absence
of references to Daniel in the apocryphal
literature of the Jews. Indeed, he himself
supplies the answer to it, for when he ap-
proaches the subject from another standpoint
he emphasises the influence which the book
exercised upon that very literature.[1] And
as for the silence of Jesus the son of Sirach,
the argument only serves to indicate the
dearth of weightier proofs. The reader can
turn to the passage referred to[2] and decide
the matter for himself. If an omission from
this panegyric of " famous men " proves anything, Ezra and the book which bears his
name must also be rejected.

The next point claims fuller notice. Daniel
was admittedly received into the canon ; but,
we are told, " it is relegated to the *Kethuvim*,

---

[1] "The book is in all respects unique, a writing *sui
generis ;* for the many imitations to which it led are but
imitations" (p. 37). This is but one of numerous instances
in which Dr. Farrar affords on one page a refutation of
objections stated upon another.

[2] *Ecclesiasticus*, xlviii. 20–xlix. 10. On this point see
Professor Margoliouth's *Lines of Defence of the Biblical
Revelation*, pp. 177, 178, 305. It is there established that
the Book of Daniel was known to Ben-Sira, and the whole
pseud-epigraph theory is thus exploded.

side by side with such a book as Esther."
The answer to this is complete. In the
Jewish canon the Old Testament Scriptures
were reckoned as twenty-four books. These
were classified as the *Torah*, the *Neveeim*,
and the *Kethuvim*—the Law, the Prophets,
and the Other Writings. Now, the objection
implies that the *Neveeim* embraced all that
was regarded as prophecy, and nothing else;
and that the contents of the *Kethuvim* were
deemed inferior to the rest of the canon.
Both these implications are false. In the
former class are placed the books of Joshua,
Judges, Samuel, and Kings. And the latter
included two books at least, than which no
part of the Scriptures was more highly
esteemed,—the Psalms, associated so inseparably with the name of King David;
and Esther, which, *pace* the sneer of the
critic, was held in exceptional honour. Dr.
Driver avers that it came to be "ranked by
the Jews as superior both to the writings of
the prophets and to all other parts of the
Hagiographa."[1]   The Psalms headed the

---

[1] *Introduction*, p. 452.

list.   Then came Proverbs, connected with
the name of Solomon.   Then Job, one of
the oldest of the books.   Then followed
the five *Megilloth* (Song of Songs, Ruth,
Lamentations, Ecclesiastes, and Esther).
And finally Daniel, Ezra and Nehemiah,
and Chronicles.   To have placed Daniel
before the *Megilloth* would have separated
it from the books with which it was so immediately associated.   In a word, its place
in the list is normal and natural.[1]

The Book of Psalms, as already mentioned, stood first in the *Kethuvim*, and in
later times gave it its name; for when our
Lord spoke of "the Law of Moses, the
Prophets, and the Psalms," he thereby
meant "all the Scriptures."[2]   Many of the
Psalms were rightly deemed prophetic; but
though David was a prophet in the highest
sense, it was not as prophet but as king that
his name was enshrined in the memory of
the people, and the book thus naturally
found its place in the third division of the

---

[1] But see p. 60, *post.*   [2] Luke xxiv. 27, 44.

canon.   For the books were grouped rather by authorship than by the character of their contents.   Precisely the same reason existed for placing Daniel where it stood; for it was not till the end of a long life spent in statecraft that the visions were accorded to the Exile.

But this is not all.   As Dr. Farrar urges, though he is obviously blind to its significance, Daniel had no claim to the prophet's mantle.   The prophets "spake as they were moved by the Holy Ghost:" *he* merely recorded the words addressed to him by the angel, and described the visions he witnessed.   And the question here, be it remembered, is not what weight would be given to this distinction by our modern critics, but how it would influence the minds of the men who settled the canon.   I am here assuming that the place which the Book of Daniel now holds in the Hebrew Bible is that which was originally assigned to it.   But this is by no means certain. There are definite reasons to suspect that it was the Talmudists who removed it from

the position it occupies in the LXX. version
and in our English Bible, and relegated it to
the third division of the canon.[1]

And now it is high time to raise a question which the critic systematically ignores,
a question which possibly he is incompetent
to deal with.   For the Higher Criticism
claims an entirely false position in this controversy.   The critic is a specialist ; and
specialists, though often necessary witnesses,
are proverbially bad judges.   To some men,
moreover, every year that passes brings
more experience in the art of weighing evidence than the theologian or the pundit
would be likely to acquire in a lifetime.
And such men are familiar with cases where
a mass of seemingly invincible proof seems
to point one way, and yet fuller inquiry
establishes that the truth lies in a wholly
opposite direction.   But the caution which
such experience begets is not to be looked
for in the critic.   And as for Dr. Farrar, his
book reminds us of a private prosecution

---

[1] On   this   subject   see   Kitto's   *Encyclopædia*,   article
"Canon," by the learned editor of that work

conducted by that type of lawyer whose remuneration is proportionate to the vehemence with which he presses every point against the defendant. It never seems to have crossed his mind that there may possibly be two sides to the question. Here, then, we have everything which can possibly be urged *against* the Book of Daniel: the inquiry remains, What further can be said in its defence? Let us call a few of the witnesses.

First comes the mention of Daniel, three times repeated, in the prophecies of Ezekiel (xiv. 14, 20, and xxviii. 3). The critics urge that a man so famous as the Daniel of the Exile is represented to have been in the book which bears his name, would have filled a large place in the literature of the nation, and they appeal to the silence of that literature in proof that no such personage in fact existed. And yet when the testimony of Ezekiel is cited, they declare that there must have been another Daniel of equal if not greater fame, who flourished at some earlier epoch of their history, albeit not even the vaguest tradition of his existence has survived! Such casuistry is hard to deal with.

But here Dr. Farrar is rash enough to leave the path so well worn by the feet of those he follows, and to venture upon a piece of independent criticism. He fixes B.C. 606 as the date of Daniel's captivity, and twelve years as his age when carried to Babylon; and he adds :—

"If Ezekiel's prophecy was uttered B.C. 584, Daniel at that time could only have been twenty-two: if it was uttered as late as B.C. 572, Daniel would still have been only thirty-four, and therefore little more than a youth in Jewish eyes. It is undoubtedly surprising that among Orientals, who regard age as the chief passport to wisdom, a living youth should be thus canonised between the Patriarch of the Deluge and the Prince of Uz."[1]

The author's words have been given *verbatim*, lest some one should charitably suppose they have been misrepresented. For the reader will perceive that this pretentious argument has no better foundation than a

---

[1] P. 10.

transparent blunder in simple arithmetic.[1]
According to his own showing, Daniel was
upwards of thirty-four,[2] and he may have
been forty-six, when Ezekiel's prophecy was
uttered.   And setting aside the absurd figment that Daniel was but a child of twelve
when deported to Babylon,[3] his age at the
date of the prophecy must, as a matter of
fact, have been forty at the least, or "if it
was uttered as late as B.C. 572," he must
have already reached middle age.   In either
case he had already attained the prime of
his powers and the zenith of his fame.

What, then, are the facts? We have
Daniel in a position of dazzling splendour
and influence at the Court of Nebuchadnezzar, second only to that of the great
king himself. His power and fame, great

---

[1] Any schoolboy can see that from B.C. 606 to B.C. 584 was
twenty-two years, and if Daniel was twelve in B.C. 606, his
age in B.C. 584 was not twenty-two, but thirty-four.   Or if
B.C. 572 was the date of the prophecy, his age when it was
uttered was forty-six.

[2] At 34 years of age Napoleon became Emperor, and the
foremost figure in Europe.   At 33, Alexander died, having
already conquered the world.

[3] Pp. 18, 19, *ante*.   If his age at the time was eighteen,
he died at eighty-eight.

though they were, cannot fail to have loomed greater still in the estimate of the humbler exiles by the river Chebar, among whom Ezekiel lived and prophesied. Neither "the Patriarch of the Deluge" nor "the Prince of Uz" would have held as large a place in the heart or in the imagination of the people. The name of their great patron must have been on every lip. His power was their security against oppression. His influence doubtless fired their hopes of a return to the land of their fathers.

Nor was this all. The college of the Chaldean Magi was famous the wide world over ; and for more than twenty years Daniel had been "chief of the wise men," and thus, in wisdom as well as in statecraft, the foremost figure of the Court of Babylon. Among Orientals, and especially among his own people, the record of the event which gained him that position, and of his triumphs of administration as Grand Vizier, would have lost nothing in the telling. And though his piety was intense and wholly phenomenal, his reputation in this respect also could not fail to be exaggerated.

Such, then, was the time and such the circumstances of Ezekiel's prophecy—words of scorn addressed to one of the great enemies of their race : " Behold thou art wiser than Daniel, there is no secret that they can hide from thee ; " or words of denunciation of the wickedness which brought such judgments upon Jerusalem : " Though these three men, Noah, Daniel, and Job, were in it, they should deliver but their own souls by their righteousness."

The refusal therefore to accept the testimony of Ezekiel as evidence to accredit the Book of Daniel is proof that neither honesty nor fairness may be looked for from the sceptics. In the judgment of all reasonable men, this single testimony will go far to decide the issue.[1]

The First Book of Maccabees is a work of the highest excellence. It has an authority and value which no other part of the Apocrypha possesses, and even Luther de-

[1] On this see also p. 98, *post.*

clared it not unworthy to be reckoned among
the sacred books of Scripture. The author
was indeed "a holy and gifted Jew," and
though the suggestion that he was no other
than John Hyrcanus is now discredited, it
gives proof of his eminence both for piety
and learning. And one of the most striking
and solemn passages of this book, the record
of the dying words of the venerable Mat-
tathias, refers to the Daniel of the Exile
and the book which bears his name.[1]

Notwithstanding the extraordinary erudition which has been brought to bear
upon this controversy, so far as I am
aware the full significance of this fact has
hitherto escaped notice. There is internal
evidence that 1 Maccabees was written before the death of John Hyrcanus (B.C. 106).
Allowing, then, for the sake of argument,
the utterly improbable hypothesis that the

---

[1] 1 Macc. ii. 59, 60. The whole passage is important, but
the special reference is to the words : "Ananias, Azarias, and
Misael by believing were saved out of the flame. Daniel for
his innocency was delivered from the mouth of the lions."
Nor is this all. The words βδέλυγμα ἐρημώσεως in 1 Macc. i.
54 are quoted from Dan. xii. 11.

canon was not closed till after the time of Antiochus, the book affords conclusive proof that among the learned of that day Daniel was regarded as the work of the great prophet-prince of the Captivity. It was as such, therefore, that it must have been admitted to the canon. The theory is thus exploded that it was as a "pseud-epigraph" that the Sanhedrim received it; and the fact of its reception becomes evidence of its genuineness which would outweigh the whole mass of the objections and difficulties which have been heaped together upon the other side.

If space were of no account, numerous points might thus be turned against the argument in support of which the critic adduces them. But these may be safely ignored in presence of other proofs of principal importance.

It was Sir Isaac Newton's opinion that "to reject Daniel's prophecies would be to undermine the Christian religion." Bishop Westcott declares that no other book of the Old Testament had so great a share in the development of Christianity.[1]   To cite a hostile witness, Professor Bevan admits that "the influence of the book is apparent almost everywhere."   In this connection he adds: "The more we realise how vast and how profound was the influence of Daniel in post-Maccabean times, the more difficult it is to believe that the book existed previously for well-nigh four centuries without exercising any perceptible influence whatsoever."[2]   On this it may be remarked, first, that it is far more difficult to believe that a "pseud-epigraph" could possibly have had an influence so vast and so profound on the development of Christianity.   The suggestion indeed, if accepted, might well discredit Christianity altogether. And secondly, it is extraordinary how any person can fail to see that the influence of the Book of Daniel in post-Maccabean times was due to the fulfilment of its predictions relating to those times.

Dr. Farrar quotes, though with special

---

[1] Smith's *Bible Dict.*, art. "Daniel."

[2] *Short Com.*, p. 15.

reprobation, the dictum of Hengstenberg, that "there are few books whose divine authority is so fully established by the testimony of the New Testament, and in particular by the Lord Himself." And yet the truth of all this no thoughtful Christian can question. St. Paul's predictions of the Antichrist point back to the visions of Daniel. And with those visions the visions of St. John—the Daniel of the New Testament—are so inseparably interwoven, that if the former be attributed to imagination, the latter must be attributed to lunacy. The Book of Daniel and the Apocalypse stand or fall together.

But the matter becomes far more serious and solemn when we realise how definitely the visions of Daniel have been adopted in the teaching of Christ. Dr. Farrar imagines that he has disposed of the matter by the figment that in the twenty-fourth chapter of Matthew the reference to "Daniel the prophet" was added by the evangelist as an explanatory note. But even if such a wild suggestion could be allowed, every intelligent reader of the passage can see that any such interpolation must have been based upon the obvious and unmistakable connection between the words of our Lord and the visions of the prophet of the Exile.

Here is a dilemma from which escape is impossible. If the Gospels be authentic and true, our Lord has adopted, and identified Himself with, the visions of this now discredited book. If the Gospels be unreliable and fictitious, the foundations of our faith are destroyed, and belief in Christianity is sheer superstition. "To the last degree dangerous, irreverent, and unwise" this may seem in the Dean of Canterbury's judgment, but its truth is none the less obvious and clear.

It cannot be asserted too plainly that Christianity is a Divine revelation. Nor need the admission be withheld that, apart from revelation in the strictest sense, the Christian's faith would be without adequate foundation. It is easy, indeed, to formulate a religious system based on the teaching of a traditional "Jesus Christ." But this is no more than a Christianised Buddhism; it is certainly not *Christianity*. The main fact on which Christianity as a system rests is the incarnation; and the man who, apart from revelation, believes in the incarnation is a credulous weak creature who would believe anything.

"The Nazarene was admittedly the son of Mary. The Jews declared that he was the son of Joseph; the Christian worships Him as the Son of God. The founder of Rome was said to be the divinely begotten child of a vestal virgin. And in the old Babylonian mysteries a similar parentage was ascribed to the martyred son of Semiramis gazetted Queen of Heaven. What grounds have we, then, for distinguishing the miraculous birth at Bethlehem from these and other kindred legends of the ancient world? To point to the resurrection is a transparent begging of the question. To appeal to human testimony is utter folly. At this point we are face to face with that to which no consensus of mere human testi-

mony could lend even an *a priori* probability."[1]

The editor of *Lux Mundi* and his allies
would here seek to save their reputation for
intelligence by setting up the authority of
"the Church" as an adequate ground for
faith. This theory, however, is a plant of
foreign growth, which, happily, has not taken
root in England. But while on this point
the Dean of Canterbury would probably re-
pudiate the teaching with which, in its de-
generate days, Pusey House identified itself,
he would doubtless endorse the words which
follow. Here is the passage :—

" The Christian creed asserts the reality of certain
historical facts. To these facts, in the Church's
name, we claim assent; but we do so on grounds
which, so far, are quite independent of the *inspiration* of the evangelical records. All that we claim
to show at this stage is that they are historical : not
historical so as to be absolutely without error, but
historical in the general sense, so as to be trustworthy. All that is necessary for faith in Christ is
to be found in the moral dispositions which predispose to belief, and make intelligible and credible the

---

[1] *A Doubter's Doubts about Science and Religion,* p. 76.

thing to be believed : coupled with such acceptance of the generally historical character of the Gospels, and of the trustworthiness of the other Apostolic documents, as justifies belief that our Lord was actually born of the Virgin Mary," &c.[1]

This language is plain enough. The gospels are not even divinely accredited as true. They are "historical *in the general sense*" indeed, and therefore as trustworthy as history in general. They afford, therefore, ample ground for belief in the public facts of the life and death of Christ. But who denies or doubts these facts? They have their place in the Koran and the writings of the Rabbis, as well as in our Christian literature. But on what ground can we justify our faith in the transcendental facts to which these public facts owe all their spiritual significance? "To these facts, in the Church's name, we claim assent," is the only reply vouchsafed to us. Let a man but yield up his judgment and bow before his priest, and he will soon acquire "the moral dispositions which predispose to belief,

---

[1] *Lux Mundi*, p. 340.

and make intelligible and credible the thing to be believed." And whether the object of his worship be Buddha or Mahomet or Christ, the result will be the same![1]

" But," Dr. Farrar here exclaims,

"Our belief in the Incarnation, and in the miracles of Christ, rests on evidence which, after repeated examination, is to us overwhelming. Apart from all questions of personal verification, or the Inward Witness of the Spirit, we can show that this evidence is supported, not only by the existing records, but by myriads of external and independent testimonies." [2]

Contempt is poured upon our belief that an angel messenger appeared to Daniel, and we are not even permitted to believe that an angel ministered to our Divine Lord in the Garden of Gethsemane.[3] But if, as the

---

[1] I have dealt with this more fully in *The Buddha of Christendom*, ch. vii.

[2] P. 40.

[3] This, according to Dr. Farrar, has no foundation save in the superstitious imagination of the three disciples when half dazed with sleep !—*The Life of Christ*, ch. lvii. What authority have we, then, for the words alleged to have been uttered by the Lord in His agony? What confidence can we feel in the narrative at all? The Gospels become (to use the critic's words about the Book of Daniel) a charming and elevating romance ! For the full development of this pro-

natural outcome of this teaching, we should be led to doubt the reality of the angelic apparition at Bethlehem, the indignation of the teacher will find vent in a scream of hysterical and unmeaning rhetoric.

For the question at issue here is the truth of the opening statement of the Gospel narrative. I allude to Matthew i. 18-25, the last verse especially. To the facts there recorded only two persons in the world could testify, and the witness of Mary and Joseph reaches us only in the very records which, we are told, are unreliable and marred by error. But Dean Farrar will assure us that, while words attributed to our Lord Himself are not to be accepted as authentic and true, the evidence here is " overwhelming." Of the reality of Joseph's visions, and of the fact of Mary's faithfulness and purity, we are supposed to have satisfied ourselves, first by "*personal* verification,"

---

fane system, see Professor Cheyne's *Encyc. Bib.*, article "Gospels." A man who accepts that article and yet professes to believe in Christianity is either utterly dishonest or hopelessly credulous and superstitious.

secondly by "the inward witness of the Spirit," thirdly by study of the "existing records"—the very records which he disparages—and lastly by "tens of thousands of external testimonies"! To discuss this is impossible, for here the writer passes out of the region in which reason holds sway, and parts company even with common-sense.

The position of the Christian is an intelligible one. Though he believes in the unseen and the unprovable, his faith is strictly rational; for, assuming a Divine revelation, belief is the highest act of reason. I cannot here discuss the grounds on which he claims to possess such a revelation.[1] I merely note the fact that the Christian maintains such a claim, and that, if it be assented to, his position is unassailable. But if once the validity of that claim be destroyed, every fearless thinker must fall back upon scepticism as "the rational attitude of a thinking mind towards the supernatural."[2]   The story

---

[1] This, of course, would raise the whole question of Inspiration, the discussion of which would be impossible here. But see p. 11, *ante*.

[2] Mill's *Essays on Religion*, p. 242.

of the Incarnation sinks at once to the level of a Galilean legend, and our faith in Christianity is the merest superstition.

Not that the removal of spurious portions of the canon need necessarily lessen faith in what remains.   But, as already urged, if the Book of Daniel be expunged the Revelation of John must share its fate, and in view of their exclusion numerous passages in the Gospels and Epistles must be fearlessly re-edited.   Some may imagine that the process, if intrusted to reverent hands, would not undermine the fabric of the Bible as a whole ; but all will admit that it could not fail to weaken it.   Nor is this plea put forward as an excuse for clinging to what is doubtful. It is designed only as a protest and a warning against the recklessness and levity of the critics.

6

"Violent Errors"

" THE existence of violent errors as to matters with which a contemporary must have been familiar, at once refutes all pretence of historic authenticity in a book professing to have been written by an author in the days and country which he describes." " By no possibility could the book have been written in the days of the Babylonian exile." Thus it is that Dean Farrar disposes of the Book of Daniel. Such dogmatism, while it will surprise and distress the thoughtful and well-informed, will no doubt overwhelm the simple folk whom this volume of the *Expositor's Bible* is presumably intended to enlighten.

Indeed, the writer betrays throughout his belief that, from Bacon to Pusey, all who have accepted the Book of Daniel as authentic have been wanting either in honesty or intelligence. And it suggests that he himself is one of a line of scholars who, as the result of independent inquiry, are agreed in rejecting it. The discovery of the hidden records of the court of Babylon cannot be much longer deferred, and when these shall have been brought to light we shall learn, perchance, on which side the folly lies—that of the believers or of the critics. And while an ignorant public is easily imposed upon by a parade of seeming scholarship, no one who is versed in the Daniel controversy can fail to recognise that fair and independent inquiry is absolutely wanting.

Porphyry the Pagan it was who set the ball rolling long ago. After resting for centuries it was again put in motion by the rationalists. And now that the fashion has set towards scepticism, and "Higher Criticism" is supposed to denote higher culture, critic follows critic, like sheep through a gap. Here in this last contribution to the controversy the writer falls into line, wholly unconscious that the "violent errors" he pillories have an existence only in the ignorance of those who denounce them. And we seek in vain for a single page that gives proof of fair and unbiassed inquiry.

But the critic will tell us that the time for inquiry is past, for the question is no longer open. " There is no shadow of doubt on the subject left in the minds of such scholars as Driver, Cheyne, Sanday, Bevan, and Robertson Smith."[1]   This list of names is intended as a climax to the pretentious periods which precede it, but this grouping together of the living and the dead makes it savour rather of anti-climax.   Do these writers monopolise the scholarship of England? or does the list represent the authorities hostile to the Book of Daniel?

It may seem ungracious to add that not one of these distinguished men has ever given proof of fitness for an inquiry so difficult and complex.   And as for the treatise here under review, every part of it gives proof of absolute unfitness for the task.   It is easy to convict an accused person if all his witnesses are put out of court and re-

---

[1] P. 118.

fused a hearing, and his own words and acts are misrepresented and distorted. Yet such is the treatment here accorded to the Book of Daniel. Not one of the champions of faith is allowed a hearing, and the exegesis offered of the prophetic portions of the book would be denounced as a mere travesty by every intelligent student of prophecy. In not a few instances, indeed, the transparent error and folly of the critic's scheme will be clear even to the ordinary reader.

Take the Seventy Weeks as an example. In adopting what he terms "the Antiochian hypothesis" of the sceptics, the critic is confronted by the fact that "it does not accurately correspond with ascertainable dates." "It is true," he says, "that from B.C. 588 to B.C. 164 only gives us 424 years, instead of 490 years." But this difficulty he disposes of by declaring that "precise computation is nowhere prevalent in the sacred books." And he adds, "to such purely mundane and secondary matters as close reckoning of dates the Jewish writers show themselves manifestly indifferent." No statement could well be more unwarrantable. A "close reckoning of dates" is almost a speciality of "Jewish writers." No other writings can compare with theirs in this respect. But let us hear what the critic has to urge.

"That there were differences of computation," he remarks, "as regards Jeremiah's seventy years, even in the age of the exile, is sufficiently shown by the different views as to their termination taken by the Chronicler (2 Chron. xxxvi. 22), who fixes it B.C. 536, and by Zechariah (Zech. i. 12), who fixes it about B.C. 519." This is his only appeal to Scripture, and, as I have already shown,[1] it is but an ignorant blunder, arising from confounding the different eras of the Servitude, the Captivity, and the Desolations.

Dr. Farrar next appeals to "exactly similar mistakes of reckoning" in Josephus, and he enumerates the following :—

"1. In his *Jewish Wars* (VI. iv. 8) he says that there were 639 years between the second year of Cyrus and the destruction of the Temple by Titus (A.D. 70). Here is an error of more than 30 years.

---
[1] Pp. 21–22, *ante.*

"2. In his *Antiquities* (XX. x.) he says that there were 434 years between the return from the Captivity (B.C. 536) and the reign of Antiochus Eupator (B.C. 164–162). Here is an error of more than 60 years.

"3. In his *Antiquities*, XIII. xi. 1, he reckons 481 years between the return from the Captivity and the time of Aristobulus (B.C. 105–104). Here is an error of some 50 years.

These "mistakes" will repay a careful scrutiny. In the passage first cited, Josephus reckons the period between the foundation of the first temple by Solomon and its destruction by Titus as 1130 years 7 months and 15 days. "And from the second building of it, *which was done by Haggai*, in the second year of Cyrus the king," the interval was 639 years and 45 days. This, be it remarked, is given as proof that "precise computation" is nowhere to be looked for in Jewish writers! The enumeration of the very days, however, renders it certain that Josephus had before him chronological tables of absolute precision. But in computing the second era above mentioned, he refers to the prophet Haggai, who, with Zechariah, promoted the building of the second temple in the second year of Darius Hystaspis. As this historian speaks elsewhere of Artaxerxes as *Cyrus*,[1] so here he calls Darius by that title. The period, therefore, was (according to our chronology) from B.C. 520 to A.D. 70— that is, 589 years—that is, about fifty years less than Josephus reckons. In Dr. Farrar's third example, this same excess of about fifty years again appears; and if in his second example we substitute 424 years for the doubtful reading of 434 years, we reach a precisely similar result.

What are we to conclude from these facts? Not that the ancient Jews were careless or indifferent in regard to chronology, which would be flagrantly untrue; but that their chronological tables, though framed with absolute precision, were marked by errors which amounted to an excess of some fifty years *in the very period to which the era of the seventy weeks must be assigned.*

Here, then, we have a solution which is

---

[1] *Ant.*, XI. vi. 1. Cyrus, like Cesar and the modern Kaiser, seems to have been used as a title.

definite and adequate of the only serious objection which the critic can urge against the application of this prophecy to Messiah. Of that application Dr. Farrar writes :—

"It is finally discredited by the fact that neither our Lord, nor His apostles, nor any of the earliest Christian writers, once appealed to the evidence of this prophecy, which, on the principles of Hengstenberg and Dr. Pusey, would have been so decisive! If such a proof lay ready to their hand—a proof definite and chronological—why should they have deliberately passed it over?"[1]

The answer is full and clear, that any such appeal would have been discredited, and any such proof refuted, by reference to what (as Josephus shows us) was the received chronology of the age they lived in. But what possible excuse can be made for those who, with the full light that history now throws upon the sacred page, not only reject its teaching, but use their utmost ingenuity to darken and distort it? "From the decree to restore Jerusalem unto the Anointed One (or 'the Messiah'), the Prince"—this, to quote Dr. Farrar's own words,[2] describes

---

[1] P. 287.   [2] P. 275.

the era here in view. There is no question that the Holy City was restored. There is no question that its restoration was in pursuance of a decree of Artaxerxes I. The date of that decree is known. From that date unto "the Messiah, the Prince," was exactly the period specified in the prophecy.[1]

But Dr. Farrar will tell us that the real epoch was not the decree to restore Jerusalem, but the catastrophe by which Jerusalem was laid in ruins. "It is obvious," he says, after enumerating "the views of the Rabbis and Fathers," "that not one of them accords with the allusions of the narrative and prayer, except that which makes the destruction of the Temple the *terminus a quo*."[2] This sort of talk is bad enough with those who seek to adapt divine prophecy to what they suppose to be the facts it refers to. But the suggestion here is that a holy and gifted *Chasid*, writing in B.C. 164, with the open page of history before him, described the *destruction* of Jerusalem as "a decree to

---

[1] See Ch. IX., *post*.
[2] Pp. 288, 289.

restore Jerusalem," and then described a
period of 424 years as 490 years! And at
the close of the nineteenth century of the
Christian era, these puerilities of the sceptics are solemnly reproduced by the Dean
of Canterbury for the enlightenment of Christian England! To escape from a difficulty
by taking refuge in an absurdity is like
committing suicide in order to escape from
danger.

Other writers tell us that the era of the
seventy weeks dated from the divine promise
recorded in Jeremiah xxix. 10.[1] But though
this view is free from the charge of absurdity
it will not bear scrutiny. That was not a
"commandment" to build Jerusalem, but
merely a promise of future restoration. All
these theories, moreover, savour of perverseness and casuistry in presence of the fact
that Scripture records so definitely the "com-

---

[1] Mr. Bevan says (*Com.*, p. 155) "the '*word*' [command-
ment] is of course" this prophecy. The force of this "of
course" is solely that this destroys the Messianic application of the angel's message! The term used is one which
occurs more than a thousand times in Scripture with many
shades of meaning, and in the Book of Esther it is repeatedly
used, as here, of the decree of a Persian king.

mandment" in pursuance of which it was in fact rebuilt.

Neither was it without significance that the prophetic period dated from the restoration under Nehemiah. The era of the Servitude had ended with the accession of Cyrus, and the seventy years of the Desolations had already expired in the second year of Darius. But the Jews were still without a constitution or a polity. In a word, their condition was then much what it is to-day. It was the decree of the twentieth year of Artaxerxes which restored the national autonomy of Judah.

And a precedent which is startling in its definiteness may be found to justify the belief that such an era would not begin while the existence of Judah as a nation was in abeyance. I allude to the 480 years of I Kings vi. I, computed from the Exodus to the Temple. If a little of the time and energy which the critics have expended in denouncing that passage as a forgery or a blunder had been devoted to searching for its hidden meaning, their labours might

perchance have been rewarded. That the
chronology of the period was correctly
known is plain from the thirteenth chapter
of the Acts, which enables us to reckon the
very same era as 573 years. How then
can this seeming error of 93 years be accounted for? *It is precisely the sum of the
several eras of the Servitudes.*[1]   The infer-

---

[1] Acts xiii. 18–21 gives 40 years in the wilderness, 450
years under the Judges, and 40 years for the reign of Saul.
To which must be added the 40 years of David's reign, and
the first three years of Solomon, for it was in his *fourth* year
that he began to build the Temple.   The servitudes were to
Mesopotamia for 8 years, to Moab for 18 years, to Canaan
for 20 years, to Midian for 7 years, and to the Philistines for
40 years. See Judges iii. 8, 14; iv. 2, 3; vi. 1; xiii. 1.
But $8+18+20+7+40$ years are precisely equal to 93 years.
To believe that this is a mere coincidence would involve
an undue strain upon our faith.

Acts xiii. 20 is one of the very many passages where the
New Testament Revisers have corrupted the text through
neglect of the well-known principles by which experts are
guided in dealing with conflicting evidence. It is certain
that neither the apostle said, nor the evangelist wrote, that
Israel's enjoyment of the land was limited to 450 years, or
that 450 years elapsed *before* the era of the Judges. The text
adopted by R.V. is therefore clearly wrong. Dean Alford
regards it "as an attempt at correcting the difficult chronology of the verse;" and he adds, "taking the words as
they stand, no other sense can be given to them than that
the time of the Judges lasted 450 years." That is, as he
explains, not that the Judges ruled for 450 years—in which
case the accusative would be used, as in verse 18—but, as

ence therefore is clear that "the 480th year" means the 480th year of national life and national responsibilities. And if this principle applied to an era apparently historical, we may *a fortiori* be prepared to find that it governs an era which is mystic and prophetic.

---

the use of the dative implies, that the period until Saul, characterised by the rule of the Judges, lasted 450 years.

The objection that I omit the servitude of Judges x. 7, 8 is met by a reference to the R.V. The punctuation of the passage in Bagster's Bible perverts the sense. That servitude affected only the tribes beyond Jordan.

7

Professor Driver's "Book of Daniel": The Evidence of the Canon

To have answered Dean Farrar's *Book of Daniel* may appear to some but a cheap and barren victory. For they will urge that if the attack on Daniel were entrusted to abler hands, the issue would be different. But the suggestion is untenable. While the passing years are bringing to light from time to time fresh evidence to confirm the authenticity of the book, the treasury of the critics is exhausted. They have no abler, no more trusted, champion than Professor Driver of Oxford; yet in his *Introduction* there is not a single count in the elaborate indictment of Daniel that will not be found in his *apparatus criticus*. And now, in his *Book of Daniel*,[1] after an

[1] *The Cambridge Bible for Schools and Colleges: The Book of Daniel*, by the Rev. S. R. Driver, D.D., Regius

interval of ten years, he has reproduced these same stock difficulties and objections, and for the most part in the same words.

That volume is fitted to excite feelings of surprise and disappointment. An "Introduction to the Literature of the Old Testament" may fitly cite what German sceptics have written on the Book of Daniel. But it is deplorable that a commentary for the use of "schools and colleges," coming from the pen of an English clergyman, a scholar of high repute, and the occupant of a chair in the University of Oxford, should be merely a modified reproduction of what German rationalism has to urge on one side of a pending controversy. Surely we might have expected some indication of independent inquiry and free thought; but we look for it in vain. The very same criticisms which Dr. Farrar has strung together are once again paraded.

Professor of Hebrew in the University of Oxford. As compared with the "Daniel" section of the *Introduction*, the only new element is the evidence of a further lapse towards the unreasoning scepticism of the "Higher Critics."

The language, of course, is very different, but the matter is for the most part identical.

Of these criticisms there is only one which is of vital importance. If, as the critics assert, there was no invasion of Judea and no deportation of Jewish captives in the third year of Jehoiakim, the historical basis upon which the Book of Daniel rests is destroyed, and the book as a whole is discredited. To that criticism, therefore, I invite the reader's close and earnest attention. If he finds it to be sustained, let him regard the controversy as closed. But if he finds it disproved by Scripture, and demonstrated to be erroneous by the strict test of chronology, let him look upon it as discrediting the critics.[1]

As for the rest of these criticisms, what Professor Driver says of some is true of them all : they will influence the mind "according as the critic, upon *independent*

---

[1] Pages 14–18, *ante*, seemed a sufficient reply to Dr. Farrar on this point. But as Dr. Driver blindly follows the same false lead, not even avoiding the blunder of the journey from Carchemish to Babylon *across the desert*, I add an excursus on the subject. See Appendix I., p. 153, *post*.

grounds, has satisfied himself that the book is the work of a later author or written by Daniel himself." If, therefore, any one of the visions of Daniel can be shown to be a Divine prophecy, the authority of the book is established. And of this, full and incontestable proof is afforded by the fulfilment of the vision of the Seventy Weeks.

The course of study which led me to these results was begun a quarter of a century ago under pressure of doubts whether the Bible could withstand the attacks of the sceptical movement known as the " Higher Criticism." In accordance with my usual habit, I set myself to test the matter by examining the critics' strongest position. For their indictment of the Book of Daniel is supposed to be unanswerable, and I confess that at first it seemed to me most formidable. But no one who has much experience of judicial inquiries is ever surprised to find that a case which seems convincing when presented *ex parte*, breaks down under cross-examination, or is shattered by opposing evidence. And this is emphatically true of the sceptical attack on Daniel.

And let it not be forgotten that the present inquiry is altogether judicial. The question involved is precisely similar in character to issues such as are daily decided in our Courts of Justice. And one of H.M. Judges with a good "special jury" would be a fitter tribunal to deal with it than any company of philologists, however eminent. Due weight would of course be given to the evidence of such men as experts. But the *dictum*, so familiar to the lawyer, would not be forgotten, that the testimony which least deserves credit is that of *skilled* witnesses, for the judgment of such men becomes warped by their habit of regarding a subject from one point of view only.[1]

The critics maintain that the definiteness of the predictions of Daniel is due to the fact that the book was written after the events referred to; and further, that its "visions" cease with the reign of Antiochus Epiphanes. The main issues of fact, there-

---

[1] Taylor's *Evidence*, Part III. Chap. V. § 1877.

fore, to be decided at such a trial would be these :—

(1) Was the Book of Daniel in existence in pre-Maccabean days? and

(2) Was any one of its visions fulfilled in later times?

And if either of these issues should be found against the critics their whole case would be shattered.

The discovery of Neptune was due to the fact that astronomers found reason to assume the existence of such a planet. And if the Book of Daniel had been lost, true criticism would assume the presence of a Daniel at the Court of Babylon. For otherwise the story of the exile and return of the Jews would be intelligible only on the assumption of miracles such as those which marked the Exodus. And further; if the advocates of the pseud-epigraph theory of Daniel were versed in the science of evidence, they would recognise that, on their own hypothesis, the presence of the book in the canon is evidence of the existence of the man. For the Sanhedrim would never have accepted it unless they had had knowledge of the historical facts on which it is based.

But while the existence of Daniel was *indisputable* when Dr. Driver wrote his *Introduction*, it was only "probable" when he came to write his *Book of Daniel*—a deplorable lapse from true criticism to "Higher Criticism," and from rational belief to unreasoning scepticism. On this point I have already cited the testimony of Ezekiel; and that testimony is conclusive unless the critics can find some adequate answer to it. The only answer they offer is not even reasonable.[1] And as regards the existence of the Book of Daniel, the same remark applies, though in a modified degree, to the testimony of 1 Maccabees.[2]

Even if the testimony of these witnesses stood alone, it would prevail with any im-

---

[1] See pp. 62–66, *ante*. In his *Lines of Defence* (p. 182) Professor Margoliouth claims to have established that a pre-Maccabean writer, Ben-Sira, "identified the Daniel mentioned by Ezekiel with the Daniel of the book that bears his name," and that he "bases a theological argument on the *last* verse of Daniel, and borrows phrases from the earlier part of the book."

[2] See pp. 66–68, *ante*.

partial tribunal. But when we come to consider the general question of the canon, the weight of proof becomes overwhelming. Apart from the disturbing influence of these controversies, no reasonable person would reject the clear and definite tradition that the completion of the Old Testament canon was the work of the men of the Great Synagogue. In an age when scepticism of a singularly shallow type has been allowed to run riot, it is the fashion to reject that tradition because of the myths and legends which have attached themselves to it. But a soberer scholarship would recognise, first, that this very element is a proof of its antiquity, and of the hold it gained upon the Jewish mind in early times ; and secondly, that if historical facts are to be ignored on this ground the whole volume of ancient history must shrink to very small proportions.

But all that concerns me here is to establish that the canon was complete before the Maccabean epoch.[1] And upon this point

---

[1] Upon the general question of the canon of the Old Testament the reader will find in Dr. Ryle's book a fair

I might almost rest the case upon the evidence of a single witness.

As mentioned in an earlier chapter,[1] *Ecclesiasticus* was written not later than about B.C. 200. The object of the book is thus explained by the grandson of the writer, who translated it into Greek not later than B.C. 132[2]: "My grandfather Jesus, seeing he had much given himself to the reading of the law, of the prophets and the other books of the Fathers, and had gotten therein sufficient proficiency, was drawn himself to write something pertaining to learning and wisdom." Now it is acknowledged

statement of the arguments in favour of a late date. And any one who is used to frequent our courts of justice will recognise the kinship of those arguments with the case which is always made against any claim to prescriptive or ancient rights. For treatises of a different kind see by all means Dr. Alexander's article on the "Canon," and Dr. Ginsburg's on the "Great Synagogue," in *Kitto's Cyclopedia;* and also Lecture VI. in Pusey's *Daniel the Prophet.*

[1] P. 52, *ante.*

[2] The evidence clearly points to an earlier date for both the book and the translation of it. But as I wish to avoid all "collateral issues." I adopt for the sake of argument the dates accepted by the critics. See, however, Dr. Ginsburg's article in *Kitto's Cyclopedia*, also Edersheim's *Life and Times of the Messiah*, vol. i. pp. 26 ff.

even by hostile critics that the words "the law and the prophets and the other books," or as he calls them again, "the rest of the books," refer to the sacred writings, and that they imply the existence at that time of a recognised canon.

"I think it quite incredible," says Dr. Ryle, "that the thrice repeated formula should have been an invention of the Greek translator, and not rather the description of the Hebrew Scriptures commonly used among the Jews."[1] *The Law, the Prophets, and the Writings*—these same words stand upon the title-page of the Jewish Bible of to-day, and no fair and competent tribunal would hesitate to find that that title has covered the same books for more than twenty-three centuries.

Ben-Sira was "a poetical paraphraser" of the Old Testament, and his book abounds in passages which are imitations of the canonical writers. And, "as clear examples of such imitation can be found of *all* the canonical books, with the doubtful exception of

---

[1] *Canon of the Old Testament* (2nd ed.), p. 313.

the Book of Daniel, these books must, as a whole, have been familiar to Ben-Sira, and must therefore be much anterior to him in date." These words are from Dr. Schechter's *Introduction*, already quoted,[1] and they are substantiated by a list of the passages referred to. That list includes three quotations from Daniel; these however are, of course, rejected by the critics.[2]

Now I confidently maintain that upon the evidence any impartial tribunal would find that the canon was complete before Ben-Sira wrote. But assuming, for the sake of argument, that the inclusion of Daniel is doubtful, the matter stands thus:—It is admitted, (1) that the canon was complete in the second century B.C.; and (2) that no book was included which was not believed to have been in existence in the days of Nehemiah.[3] For the test by which a book was admitted to the canon was its claim to

---

[1] P. 54, *ante* (the quotation is from p. 35).

[2] Hence Dr. Schechter's expression, "the doubtful exception of Daniel." He himself doubts, not the quotations from Daniel, but the "exception" maintained by the critics.

[3] Dr. Ryle, *Canon of the Old Testament*, pp. 175 and 188.

be inspired; and the Sanhedrim held that inspiration ceased with the prophets, and that no "prophet"—that is, no divinely inspired teacher—had arisen in Israel after the Nehemiah era.[1]   When, therefore, Josephus declares that the Scriptures were "justly believed to be Divine," and that the Jews were prepared "willingly to die for them,"[2] he is not recording merely the opinion of his contemporaries, but the settled traditional belief of his nation.

How, then, can the critics reconcile their hypothesis as to the origin of the Book of Daniel with its inclusion in the canon?

As regards point (1) above indicated, the Bishop of Exeter's testimony carries with it the special authority which attaches to the statements of a hostile witness. "If," he says, "all the books of 'the Kethubim' were known and received in the first century A.D., and if, as we believe, the circumstances of the Jewish people rendered it all but impos-

---

[1] The question of the justice of such beliefs and claims in no way affects the force of my argument.

[2] *Against Apion*, i. 8.

sible for the canon to receive change or
augmentation in the first century B.C., we
conclude that ' the disputed books ' received a
recognition in the last two or three decades of
the second century B.C., when John Hyrcanus
ruled and the Jews still enjoyed prosperity."

This ought to decide the whole question.
For mark what it means.   The critics would
have us believe that after the death of Antiochus some Jewish *Chasid* incorporated a history of his reign in a historical romance,
casting it into the form of a prophecy supposed to have been delivered hundreds of
years before ; and that, at a time when this
was still a matter within living memory,
the work was accepted as divinely inspired
Scripture, and bracketed with the Psalms
of David among the sacred books of the
Hebrew nation !

We are dealing here, remember, with the
acts, not of savages in a barbarous age, but
of the religious leaders of the Jews in historic times.   And the matter in question related to the most solemn and important of
all their duties.   Moreover, the Sanhedrim

of the second century B.C. was composed of
men of the type of John Hyrcanus ; men
famed for their piety and learning ; men who
were heirs of all the proud traditions of the
Jewish faith, and themselves the sons or suc-
cessors of the heroes of the noble Maccabean
revolt.   And yet we are asked to believe
that these men, with their extremely strict
views of inspiration and their intense reverence for their sacred writings—that these
men, the most scrupulous and conservative
Church body that the world has ever known
—used their authority to smuggle into the
sacred canon a book which, *ex hypothesi*, was
a forgery, a literary fraud, a religious novel
of recent date.

Such a figment is worthy of its pagan
author, but it is wholly unworthy of Christian men in the position of English ecclesi-
astics and University Professors.   And were
it not for the glamour of their names it would
be deemed undeserving of notice.   But our
respect for Church dignitaries of our own
times must not make us forget what is due
to the memory of Church dignitaries of

another age, men whose fidelity to their trust as the divinely appointed custodians of "the oracles of God" has earned for them the gratitude and admiration of the Church for all time. Their fitness, moreover, to judge of the genuineness and authenticity of the Book of Daniel was incomparably greater than could be claimed for any of those who join in this base and silly slander upon their intelligence or their honesty. For if the critics are right, these men who were, I repeat, the divinely appointed custodians of the Hebrew Scriptures,[1] and from whom the Christian Church has received them, were no better than knaves or fools. Let no one start at this language, for it is not a whit too strong. They were utter fools if they were deceived by a literary forgery of their own time; they were shameless knaves if they shared in a plot to secure the acceptance of the fraud.

For let it be kept steadily in view that no book would have been thus honoured unless it was believed to be ancient. The "avowed

---

[1] Rom. iii. 2.

fiction" theory of Daniel is puerile in its absurdity.[1] If the book was not genuine it was a forgery palmed off upon the Sanhedrim. And like all forgeries of that kind the MS. must have been "discovered" by its author. But the "finding" of such a book at such a period of the national history would have been an event of unparalleled interest and importance. Where then is the record of it? When it suits them, the critics make great use of the argument from the *silence* of witnesses; but in a case like this where that argument has overwhelming force they ignore it altogether.

Moreover, the suggestion of the critics that the Sanhedrim admitted a book to the canon in the way a library committee adds a volume to their catalogue is grotesque in the extreme. "They never determined a book to be canonical in the sense of intro-

---

[1] Imagine a meeting of the upper House of Convocation to discuss a proposal to add Dr. Farrar's *Life of Christ* to the canon of the New Testament! Quite as grotesquely ridiculous is the suggestion that the Jewish Sanhedrim in the second century B.C. would have entertained the question of adding "an elevating romance" of their own age to the canon of the Old Testament.

ducing it into the canon.   In every instance
in which a writing is said to have been
admitted to the canon, the writing had
already been in existence for generations,
and had for generations been claimed as
canonical before the discussions arose in
regard to it.   In every instance the decision
is not that the book shall now be received
into the collection of sacred writings, but that
the evidence shows it to have been regarded
from the first as a part of that collection."[1]

One point more.   While books of great
repute, such as Ecclesiasticus and 1 Maccabees, were absolutely excluded from the
canon, and even canonical books, such as
the Book of Proverbs, Ecclesiastes, and
even Ezekiel were challenged, "*the right
of the Book of Daniel to canonicity was never
called in question in the Ancient Synagogue.*"[2]

In disparagement of Daniel the critics
point to the extraordinary additions which
mark the Septuagint version.   But owing to

---

[1] *Encyc. Americana,* article "Bible."

[2] Edersheim's *Life and Times of the Messiah,* vol. ii.,
App. V.

their want of experience in dealing with evidence, they fail to see what signal proof this affords of the antiquity of the book. The critics themselves allow that the Greek version of Daniel was in existence before 1 Maccabees was written.[1] According to their own case, therefore, the interval between the appearance of the book and its translation into Greek must have been within the memory of the older members of the Sanhedrim. And yet they ask us to believe that though during that interval it was under consideration for admission to the canon, it was guarded so carelessly that these additions and corruptions were allowed.[2] The Septuagint version is evidence that Daniel was a pre-Maccabean work : the corruptions of the text which mark that version are evidence that it was in existence long before the Maccabean era.

---

[1] The presumption is strong that the LXX. version was in existence at the date to which the critics assign the book itself. But here, as on every other point, I am arguing the question on bases accepted by the critics themselves.

[2] And Professor Cheyne adopts the suggestion that the Hebrew original of ii. 14 to vii. was allowed to be lost ! (Smith's *Bible Dict.*, art. " Daniel ").

In view of all this it is not surprising that even a writer so cautious and so fair as Canon Girdlestone should assert that "there is not an atom of ground for the supposition that any of the books or parts of books which constitute our Old Testament were the work of men of that age." "Of one thing," he adds, "we may be quite certain: nothing would be introduced into the 'Sacred Library' which was not believed to be 'prophetic,' and therefore in some sense Divine, and though there were occasionally men after Nehemiah's time who had semi-prophetic gifts, the Jews do not acknowledge them as prophets.[1] . . . We look in vain down the remains and traditions of Hebrew history between the age of Nehemiah and the Christian era for the appearance of any men who would venture to add to or take from the sacred library or canon which existed in Nehemiah's days."[2]

Upon the first of the issues above specified

---

[1] In proof of this he refers to 1 Maccabees iv. 46; ix. 27 (which puts the prophets in the far past); and xiv. 41.

[2] *The Foundations of the Bible*, ch. ii., pp. 8 and 10.

I therefore claim a decision in favour of the Book of Daniel. I now proceed to state the grounds upon which, with equal confidence, I claim a verdict also on the second.

8

The Vision of the "Seventy Weeks": The Prophetic Year

As the solution of the problem of the Seventy Weeks is my personal contribution to the Daniel controversy, I may be pardoned for dealing with the subject here in greater detail, albeit this involves some repetition. It is all the more necessary, moreover, because in his recent work Professor Driver has adopted the laboured efforts of the foreign sceptics to evade the Messianic reference of the vision. Indeed, his exposition of the passage reminds us of that sort of dream in which words never have their natural meaning and events always happen in some unexpected way.

In the ninth chapter of Daniel the scene is laid in Babylon, and the occasion is the approaching end of the " Desolations," an

era which the critics without exception con-
found with either the "Servitude" or the
"Captivity."[1] "I Daniel," the writer tells
us, "understood by the books the number
of the years whereof the word of the Lord
came to Jeremiah the prophet for the accom-
plishing of the desolations of Jerusalem, even
seventy years."[2] Then follows the record
of his passionately earnest prayer on behalf
of his city and his people,[3] which prayer
brings in answer the angel's message. Here
is the text of Dan. ix. 24–27 (R.V.)[4]:—

"Seventy weeks are decreed upon thy people
and upon thy holy city, to finish transgression and
to make an end of sins and to make reconciliation
for iniquity and to bring in everlasting righteousness and to seal up vision and prophecy and to
anoint the most holy. Know therefore and discern
that from the going forth of the commandment to
restore and to build Jerusalem unto the anointed
one (or Messiah) the prince shall be seven weeks
and threescore and two weeks: it shall be built
again with street and moat, even in troublous times.

---

[1] See pp. 21, 22, *ante.*
[2] Ver. 2.   [3] Ver. 19.
[4] As to the punctuation of this passage, see Appendix
III., p. 167, *post.*

And after the threescore and two weeks shall the anointed one (or Messiah) be cut off and shall have nothing: and the people of the prince that shall come shall destroy the city and the sanctuary; and his end shall be with a flood, and even unto the end shall be war; desolations are determined. And he shall make a firm covenant with many for one week: and for the half of the week he shall cause the sacrifice and the oblation to cease."

Well may Professor Driver and Dean Farrar comment upon the hopeless divergence which marks "the bewildering mass of explanations" offered by the numberless expositors of this passage.   But there is no reason why the intelligent reader should follow these eminent critics who, in their "bewilderment," have adopted the most preposterous interpretation of it ever proposed. For such indeed is the suggestion that any devout Jew—whether the prophet of the Exile or a Maccabean zealot, it matters not which—could thus anticipate "the complete redemption of Israel"[1] apart from the advent of Messiah.   It is absolutely certain that the vision points to the coming of Christ,

---

[1] The words are Professor Driver's (*Daniel*, p. 135).

and any other view of it is indeed " a resort of desperation."

May I now invite my reader to follow me in the path which I myself have traversed in seeking the explanation of the vision? Rejecting all mystical or strained interpretations, let him insist on taking the words in their simple and obvious meaning ; and with the help of a key which, though long overlooked, is ready at hand, he will find the solution, full and clear, of what may have seemed a hopeless enigma.

Here was a man trained by his Scriptures to look for a Messiah whose advent would bring fulness of blessing to his people and city.[1] But his people were in captivity and his city was in ruins. And having himself already passed the allotted span of life, he could not hope to outlive the period of the Divine judgment of the Desolations, of which some seventeen years were still unexpired. So he set himself to plead for light ; and the answer came that the realisation of the pro-

---

[1] With those who regard the Book of Daniel as a pseud-epigraph my argument here should have special force.

mised Messianic blessings was deferred until the close of an era of seven times the seventy years of the Desolations—not seventy years, but "seventy weeks" of years.[1]

These seventy weeks, moreover, were divided thus—7 + 62 + 1. The period "unto Messiah the prince" was to be "seven weeks and threescore and two weeks;" and at the close of the middle era—"after the threescore and two weeks"—Messiah was to be "cut off." In other words, the presentation and rejection of Messiah were to be 69 weeks, or 483 years, from the epoch of the era.

The first question, then, which claims attention is the character of the year of which this prophetic era is composed. Here expositor after expositor and critic after critic has held in his hand the key to the whole problem, but has thrown it away unused.

---

[1] With the Jew the effect of his laws was "to render the word week capable of meaning a seven of years almost as naturally as a seven of days. Indeed the generality of the word would have this effect at any rate. Hence its use to denote the latter in prophecy is not mere arbitrary symbolism, but the employment of a not unfamiliar and easily understood language."—Smith's *Bib. Dict.*, art. "Week."

All are agreed that the "seventy weeks" of verse 24 are seven times the seventy years of verse 2; if, then, the duration of the seventy years of the Desolations can be ascertained, the problem is solved.

Seventy years was the appointed duration of the Servitude to Babylon.[1] But the stubborn refusal of the people to submit to that judgment,[2] or to profit by the further chastisement of the Captivity, which followed eight or nine years afterwards, brought on them the terrible scourge of the Desolations.[3] The essential element in this last judgment was not merely ruined cities, but a land laid desolate by a hostile invasion, the effects of which were perpetuated by famine and pestilence, the continuing proofs of the Divine displeasure.[4] The Desolations, therefore, were reckoned from the day the capital

---

[1] Jer. xxix. 10, and note the R.V. "*for* (not *at*) Babylon." The figment of a seventy years' captivity, though so generally held, is a blunder. The Captivity lasted only sixty-two years.

[2] Jer. xxvii. 6, 17 ; xxviii. 14.

[3] This was foretold in the fourth year of Jehoiakim, after the Servitude had began (Jer. xxv. 1–11).

[4] Jer. xxvii. 13 ; Hag. ii. 17.

was invested, the 10th day of the 10th month in the ninth year of Zedekiah.[1] This was the epoch of the judgment as revealed to the prophet Ezekiel in his exile;[2] and for four-and-twenty centuries it has been observed as a fast by the Jews in every land.

As an interval of seventeen years elapsed between the epoch of the Servitude and that of the Desolations, so by seventeen years the second period overlapped the first. And this explains the seemingly inexplicable fact that a few refractory Samaritans were allowed to thwart the execution of the work expressly ordered by the edict of Cyrus. Until the era of the Desolations had run its course the Divine judgment which rested upon the land vetoed the rebuilding of the sacred Temple.

As the epoch of that era is recorded with absolute definiteness, so also is its close. It ended upon the 24th day of the 9th month in the second year of Darius Hystaspis of

---

[1] 2 Kings xxv. 1 ; Jer. lii. 4.   The event, of course, put an end to all agricultural pursuits.

[2] Ezek. xxiv. 1, 2.

Persia. The reader will do well here to peruse the prophecy of Haggai and the first chapter of Zechariah. I will quote but a single sentence of each: "Then the angel of the Lord answered and said, O Lord of hosts, how long wilt Thou not have mercy on Jerusalem and on the cities of Judah, against which Thou hast had indignation these threescore and ten years?"[1] "Consider now from this day and upward, from the four-and-twentieth day of the ninth month, even from the day that the foundation of the Lord's temple was laid, consider it. . . . *From this day will I bless you.*"[2]

Now the Julian date of the 10th day of the 10th month in the ninth year of Zedekiah was the 15th December, B.C. 589; and that of the 24th day of the 9th month in the second year of Darius Hystaspis was the 17th December, B.C. 520. The intervening period, therefore, was exactly sixty-nine years. But sixty-nine years contain 25,200 days, the precise

---

[1] Zech. i. 12.

[2] Hag. ii. 18, 19; compare Ezra iv. 24; v. 1, 2.

equivalent of seventy years of 360 days.[1]
It is clear, therefore, that, as the era of
the Desolations was a Divine judgment
upon Judah, the period was measured with
all the accuracy of a judicial sentence.

Even if this stood alone it would be
conclusive. But, further, we are expressly
told that the era of the Desolations was
fixed at seventy years, because of the
neglect of the Sabbatic years.[2] Therefore
we might expect to find that a period of
70×7 years, measured back from the
end of the Desolations, would bring us to
the time when Israel entered into their
full national privileges, and thus incurred

---

[1] $365\frac{1}{4} \times 69 = 25,200$, and $360 \times 70 = 25,200$. I may here
explain that in giving historical dates I follow secular
historians and chronologists, and not writers on prophecy,
who are too prone to "cook" the chronology to suit their
schemes of interpretation. In the above instance I follow
Clinton, but with this difference—that he wrote in ignorance
of the *Mishna* rule that a king's reign was always reckoned
from Nisan (see App. IV., *post*). The thirty-seventh year
of the Captivity, reckoned from the eighth year of Nebuchadnezzar, was the first year of Evil-Merodach (2 Kings
xxv. 27), *i.e.* 561, and that date fixes the whole chronology,
as Clinton shows (*Fasti Hel.*, vol. i. p. 319). Zedekiah's
reign, therefore, dates from Nisan, B.C. 597, and not 598.

[2] 2 Chron. xxxvi. 21 ; *cf.* Lev. xxvi. 34, 35.

their full responsibilities. And such, in fact, will be found to be the case. From the year after the dedication of Solomon's temple to the year before the foundation of the second temple was a period of 490 years of 360 days.[1]

But even this is not all. No one doubts that the visions of the Revelation refer to the visions of Daniel, and for this purpose they may be read together. And there we find a part of the prophetic era sub-divided into the days of which it is com-posed. Half of one week of the vision is twice described as forty-two months;[2] and twice as 1260 days.[3] But 1260 days are exactly equal to forty-two months of thirty days, or three and a half years of 360 days.

To English ears the suggestion may seem fanciful that a chronological era should be

---

[1] The temple was dedicated in the eleventh year of Solomon (B.C. 1005). The Desolations ended, as above stated, in the second year of Darius Hystaspis (B.C. 520). The intervening period, reckoned *exclusively*, was 483 years, or 70 × 7 luni-solar years of 360 days.

[2] Rev. xi. 2 ; xiii. 5.

[3] Rev. xi. 3 ; xii. 6.

reckoned thus in luni-solar years.   But it was not so with those for whom the prophecy was given.   Such, it is reasonably certain, was the form of year then in use both at Babylon and at Jerusalem.   Such was in fact the year of the Noachian age.[1]   Tradition testifies that it was the year which Abraham knew in his Chaldean home, and which was afterwards preserved in his family. And Sir Isaac Newton avers that

"All nations, before the just length of the solar year was known, reckoned months by the course of the moon, and years by the return of winter and summer, spring and autumn ; and in making calendars for their festivals, they reckoned thirty days to a lunar month, and twelve lunar months to a year, taking the nearest round numbers, whence came the division of the ecliptic into 360 degrees."

And in quoting this statement, Sir G. C. Lewis declares that

"All credible testimony and all antecedent probability lead to the result that a solar year containing

---

[1] 150 days being specified as the interval between the 17th day of the 2nd month and the 17th day of the 7th month (Gen. vii. 11 ; viii. 3, 4).

twelve lunar months, determined within certain limits of error, has been generally recognised by the nations adjoining the Mediterranean from a remote antiquity." [1]

In view of all this mass of cumulative proof, the conclusion may be regarded as raised above the sphere of controversy or doubt, that the prophetic year is not the Julian year of 365¼ days, but the ancient year of 360 days.

---

[1] *Astronomy of the Ancients*, ch. i. § 7.

9

The Fulfillment of the Vision of the "Weeks"

In view of the proofs adduced in the preceding chapter, it may now be accepted as a demonstrated fact that the unit of the prophetic era of the seventy weeks is the lunisolar year of the ancient world. Our next inquiry must be directed to ascertaining the epoch of that era.

The language of the vision is simple and clear: "From the going forth of the commandment to restore and to build Jerusalem unto Messiah the Prince, shall be seven weeks and threescore and two weeks." Here at least we might suppose that no question could arise. But with Professor Driver, following the lead of the wildest and worst of the foreign sceptical expositors, "the commandment to rebuild Jerusalem" becomes the prophecy that Jerusalem would be rebuilt;

"Messiah, the Prince" becomes Cyrus, King of Persia;[1] and by a false punctuation which divides the sentence in the middle,[2] the sixty-two weeks become the period for which the city was to be restored. I appeal to the reader to reject this nightmare system of interpretation, and to follow the early fathers and the best of the modern expositors in accepting the words in their plain and natural meaning.

What then was the "commandment," or edict, or *firman* to build Jerusalem? The Book of Ezra records three several decrees of Persian kings, relating to the Jews. The opening verses record the edict of Cyrus, which authorised the return of the exiles. But this decree mentioned only the temple and not the city; and moreover it referred to the era of the Servitude, and not of the Desolations, which later era it was that Daniel had in view.[3] The sixth chapter

---

[1] Albeit the vision was given in 538 B.C., and the restoration under Cyrus was in 536!

[2] See Appendix III., p. 167.

[3] Canon Rawlinson assumes that the temple was fifteen years in building (*Five Great Men*, iv. 398). But this is vetoed by Scripture. Ezra iii. 8-11 records that the founda-

records a decree issued by Darius Hystaspis to confirm the decree of Cyrus, but this in no way extended the scope of the earlier edict. The seventh chapter records a third decree, issued by Artaxerxes Longimanus in his seventh year, but this again related merely to the temple and its worship.[1] The Book of Ezra therefore will be searched in vain for what we seek, but the book which follows it gives it fully and explicitly.

The Book of Nehemiah opens by relating that while at Susa, where he was in attendance as cupbearer to the king, "an honour of no small account in Persia,"[2] he learned from certain of his brethren who had just arrived from Judea that the Jews there were "in great affliction and reproach;" "the wall of Jerusalem also was broken down, and the gates thereof were burned with fire."[3] The next chapter relates that while discharging

---

tion was then laid, but though the *altar* was set up and sacrifices renewed (iii. 3, 6), the *foundation* was again laid fifteen years later, for not a stone of the house had yet been placed (Hag. ii. 10, 15, 18).

[1] Ezra vii. 19, 27.   [2] *Herodotus*, iii. 34.

[3] Neh. i. 2, 3.

the duties of his high office, Artaxerxes noticed his distress, and called for an explanation of it. "Let the king live for ever," Nehemiah answered, "why should not my countenance be sad, when the city, the place of my fathers' sepulchres, lieth waste, and the gates thereof are burned with fire?" "For what dost thou make request?" the king demanded. To which Nehemiah answered, "That thou wouldest send me unto Judah, unto the city of my fathers' sepulchres, THAT I MAY BUILD IT."[1] Artaxerxes forthwith granted the petition, and issued an edict to give effect to it. This occurred in the beginning of the Jewish year; and before the Feast of Tabernacles, in the seventh month, Jerusalem was once more a city, enclosed by gates and ramparts.

Of course there must have been many streets of inhabited houses in Jerusalem ever since the first return of the exiles. But, as Dr. Tregelles justly says,[2] "the very existence of the place *as a city* depended upon such a decree" as that of the twentieth

---

[1] Neh. ii. 5.   [2] *Daniel*, p. 98.

year of Artaxerxes.   Once, at an earlier
period, work which the Jews were executing
under the decree of Cyrus had been stopped
on the false charge that its design was to
restore *the city*.   " A rebellious city " it had
ever proved, the local officials declared in
reporting to the king ; and they added, "*If
this city be builded, and the walls thereof set
up again,* by this means thou shalt have no
portion on this side the river."[1]   The edict
of Cyrus was in keeping with the general
policy of toleration, to which the inscriptions
bear testimony : it was a wholly different
matter to allow the conquered race to set up
again the famous fortifications of Jerusalem,
and to restore under Nehemiah the old polity
of the Judges.   This was a revival of the
political existence of Judah ; and therefore
no doubt it was that the event was divinely
chosen as the beginning of the prophetic
era of the seventy weeks.[2]

---

[1] *i.e.* Euphrates.   Ezra iv. 16–22.

[2] For the same reason, *e.g.*, the "Servitudes" were
ignored in reckoning the time of Israel's national responsibilities (see p. 90, *ante*).

This sudden change in the policy of the Persian court was

It is certain, moreover, that this edict of Artaxerxes is the only " commandment to restore and build Jerusalem" recorded in history, and that under this " commandment" Jerusalem was in fact rebuilt. Unless, therefore, the nightmare system of interpretation must prevail, we may accept it, not as a plausible theory or a happy guess, but as a definite fact, that the seventy weeks are to be computed from the date of the issuing of this decree.

The date of it is expressly recorded by Nehemiah. It was made in the beginning of the Jewish year in the twentieth year of the king's reign. And the Julian date of the first Nisan in the twentieth year of Artaxerxes is the 14th March B.C. 445.[1] Here let me quote the words of the vision once again. " From the going forth of the commandment to restore and build

---

not due merely to the influence of a popular minister. In his *History of the Jews*, Dean Milman accounts for it by "the foreign history of the times." The terms imposed on Persia by the victorious Athenians seem to have rendered it important to make Jerusalem a fortified city.

[1] See App. V., p. 179, *post.*

Jerusalem unto Messiah the Prince shall be seven weeks and threescore and two weeks. . . . And after the threescore and two weeks shall the Messiah be cut off." [1]

If, therefore, the vision be a Divine prophecy, an era of " sixty-nine weeks," that is, of 483 prophetic years, reckoned from the 14th March B.C. 445, should close with the public presentation and death of " Messiah the Prince."

No student of the Gospels can fail to see that the Lord's last visit to Jerusalem was not only in fact but in intention the crisis of His ministry. From the time that the accredited leaders of the nation had rejected His Messianic claims, He had avoided all public recognition of those claims. But now His testimony had been fully given, and the purpose of His entry into the capital was to openly proclaim His Messiahship and to receive His doom. Even His apostles themselves had again and again been charged that

---

[1] *Not* "after sixty-two weeks"—which might mean sixty-two weeks reckoned from the beginning of the era—but "after *the* sixty-two weeks" which follow the seven : *i.e.* at the close of the sixty-ninth week of the era.

they should not make Him known ; but now
He accepted the acclamations of " the whole
multitude of the disciples." And when the
Pharisees protested, He silenced them with
the indignant rebuke, " I tell you that if
these should hold their peace the stones
would immediately cry out." [1]   These words
can only mean that the divinely appointed
time had arrived for the public announcement of His Messiahship, and that the Divine
purpose could not be thwarted.

The full significance of the words which
follow is lost in our Authorised Version. As
the cry was raised by His disciples, " Ho-
sanna to the Son of David, blessed is the
King of Israel that cometh in the name of
the Lord," He looked off towards the Holy
City and exclaimed, " If *thou* also hadst
known, even ON THIS DAY, the things that
belong to thy peace—but now they are hid
from thine eyes ! " [2]   The nation had already

---

[1] Luke xix. 39, 40.

[2] R.V. reads, " If thou hadst known *in this day* " ; A.V.
reads, " this *thy* day."   Alford's note is, " thou also, as well
as these My disciples."   And so also the *Speaker's Commentary.*

rejected Him, but this was the fateful day when their decision must be irrevocable. And we are expressly told that it was the fulfilment of the prophecy, "Shout, O daughter of Jerusalem ; behold thy King cometh unto thee." [1]   It was the only occasion on which His kingly claims were publicly announced. And no other day in all His ministry will satisfy the words of Daniel's vision. [2]

And the date of that first " Palm Sunday " can be ascertained with certainty.   No year in the whole field of ancient history is more definitely indicated than that of the beginning of our Lord's public ministry.   According to the Evangelist it was "the fifteenth year of Tiberius Cæsar." [3]   Now "the reign of Tiberius, as beginning from 19th August, A.D. 14, was as well known a date in the time of Luke as the reign of Queen Victoria is in

---

[1] Zech. ix. 9 ; Matt. xxi. 4, 5.

[2] The only other possible day would be either the day of His birth or the first day of His public ministry.   But neither date is recorded.   As regards the nativity, the only thing reasonably certain is, that it occurred neither in the year nor on the day to which it is popularly assigned.

[3] Luke iii. 1.

our own day."[1] The Evangelist, moreover, with a prophetic anticipation of the perverseness of expositors and "reconcilers," goes on to name six prominent public men as holding specified positions in the fifteenth year of Tiberius, and each one of these is known to have actually held the position thus assigned to him in the year in question.

As, therefore, the first Passover of the Lord's ministry was that of Nisan, A.D. 29, the date of the Passion is thus fixed by Scripture itself. For it is no longer necessary to offer proof that the crucifixion took place at the fourth Passover of the ministry. According to the Jewish custom, our Lord went up to Jerusalem on the 8th Nisan,[2] which, as we know, fell that year upon a Friday. And having spent the Sabbath at Bethany, He entered the Holy City the following day, as recorded in the Gospels.

The Julian date of that 10th Nisan was

---

[1] Lewin, *Fasti Sacri*, p. liii. He adds, "And no single case can be produced in which the years of Tiberius were reckoned in any other manner."

[2] John xi. 55, xii. 1 ; Josephus, *Wars*, vi. 5, 3.

Sunday the 6th April, A.D. 32.[1]   What then was the length of the period intervening between the issuing of the decree to rebuild Jerusalem and this public advent of " Messiah the Prince"—between the 14th March, B.C. 445, and the 6th April, A.D. 32 ?   THE INTERVAL WAS EXACTLY AND TO THE VERY DAY 173,880 DAYS, OR SEVEN TIMES SIXTY-NINE PROPHETIC YEARS OF 360 DAYS.[2]

---

[1] See Appendices IV., p. 171 and VI., p. 176, *post.*

[2] From B.C. 445 to A.D. 32 is 476 years = 173,740 days $(476 \times 365) + 116$ days for leap years.   And from 14th March to 6th April (reckoned inclusively according to Jewish practice) is 24 days.   But $173,740 + 116 + 24 = 173,880$.   And $69 \times 7 \times 360 = 173,880$.

It must be borne in mind here that in reckoning years from B.C. to A.D. *one* year must always be omitted ; for, of course, the interval between B.C. 1 and A.D. 1 is not *two* years but one year.   In fact B.C. 1 ought to be called B.C. 0 ; and it is so described by astronomers, with whom B.C. 445 is -444 (see App. V., p. 174, *post*).   And again, as the Julian year is 11 m. 10.46 s., or about the 129th part of a day, longer than the mean solar year, the Julian calendar has three leap years too many in every four centuries.   This error is corrected by the Gregorian reform, which reckons three *secular* years out of four as common years.   For instance, 1700, 1800, and 1900 were common years, and 2000 will be a leap year.

10

Summary and Conclusion

IT will be obvious to the intelligent and thoughtful that unless the conclusions recorded in the preceding chapter can in some way be disproved or got rid of, there is an end of the Daniel controversy. The reader, therefore, will be interested to know what reply Professor Driver has to give to them.

After noticing the solution of the Seventy Weeks proposed by Julius Africanus, the father of Christian chronologers,[1] he proceeds :—

"This view has been revived recently, in a slightly modified form, by Dr. Robert Anderson, according to whom the 'year' of Daniel was the ancient luni-solar year of 360 days; reckoning, then, 483 years (=69 'weeks'), of 360 days each, from 1 Nisan, B.C. 445, the date of the edict of

---

[1] About A.D. 200.

Artaxerxes, Dr. Anderson arrives at the 10th of
Nisan in the 18th year of Tiberius Cæsar, the day on
which our Lord made His public entry into Jerusalem (Luke xix. 37 ff.).   Upon this theory, however, even supposing the objections against B.C. 445
as the *terminus a quo* to be waived, the seventieth
week remains unexplained."

There is one objection, I admit, to the B.C.
445 date; it violates the canon of interpretation, that Scripture never means what it says!
But waiving that point, the only criticism
which the highest scholarship has to offer
upon my scheme is that it leaves the seventieth week "unexplained."

This objection would be irrelevant even if
it were well founded.   But as a matter of
fact the book to which Dr. Driver refers
his readers deals fully and in much detail
with the seventieth week.[1]   One of the
blunders of this controversy is that of sup-

---

[1] His reference is to *The Coming Prince, or the Seventy
Weeks of Daniel*, 5th ed.   The first edition of the book
appeared in 1881 : the ninth is now current.   The scheme
has thus been before the public for many years; and during
that time every detail of it has been subjected to the most
searching criticism, both here and in America; but neither
error nor flaw has been detected in it.

posing that the era of the seventy weeks was to end either with the advent or the death of Christ.   Here the language of Daniel is explicit : the period "unto Messiah the Prince" was to be, not seventy weeks, but sixty-nine weeks.   The crucifixion is the event which marks the end of the sixty-ninth week ; the seventieth week ends with the restoration of the Jews to prosperity and blessing.   Those who regard that week as cancelled hold an intelligible position.   And the same may be said of those who maintain that it still awaits fulfilment.   But the figment that a prophecy of temporal and spiritual good for the Jews was fulfilled by their rejection and ruin is one of the very wildest vagaries of interpretation.[1]

Upon this point three different opinions prevail.   By some the restoration of the Jews is dismissed as a dream of Hebrew poetry.   Others consider that the Jewish

---

[1] Another amazing vagary of the same type is that Dan. ix. 27 means that our Lord made some sort of seven years' covenant with the Jews at the beginning of His ministry, and that it was broken by His death.   See *The Coming Prince*, ch. xiv., and especially pp. 182, 183.

promises were finally forfeited by the rejection of Christ, and now belong to the Gentile Church. And others again are bold enough to believe that God will make good every promise and every prophecy the Bible contains, but that the realisation of the distinctive blessings of the favoured nation is postponed until the close of this Gentile dispensation. I am not ashamed to rank myself in this third category ; and following the teaching of the Ante-Nicene Fathers—for this is precisely the sort of question as to which apostolic tradition is least likely to have been corrupted—to hold that the seventieth week, and the events pertaining to it, belong to the future.

But what bearing has all this upon the point at issue ? The question here is whether the vision of the seventy weeks was a mere human prediction or a Divine prophecy. The popular view of the matter appears to be that, as the advent of Christ was expected about the time when He actually appeared, there was nothing extraordinary in a chronological forecast of the event. But this betrays a strange misconception and confusion of thought.

True it is that the advent of their Messiah was a hope universally cherished by the Jews —a fact which, as I have urged, proves the error and folly of denying the Messianic interpretation of the 9th of Daniel. But if His coming was expected nineteen centuries ago, the hope was based on these very visions. For, apart from Daniel, Scripture contains no hint of a time limit within which the advent was to take place. Apart from Daniel, indeed, the theory was plausible that it would herald the dawn of the seventh millennium of the world's history—an epoch which, by the Jewish calendar, is even now in the distant future. But here is a book which specifies the precise date of the presentation and death of Christ, and the prediction has been fulfilled. Had it been fulfilled within the year, the result might well stagger unbelief. And if the apparent margin of error had been a month, the explanation would be obvious and adequate, that Nehemiah does not record the day of the month on which the edict was signed.[1]   But, as a matter of fact, it was fulfilled with absolute accuracy, and to the very day.

Let us for a moment ignore the controversy about the date of Daniel—whether in the second century B.C., or in the sixth, and confine our attention to this simple issue: Could the prediction have been a mere guess by some learned and pious Jew? If we refer this question to a mathematician he will ask what data there were to work upon; and on hearing that there were none, he will tell us that in such circumstances the chance of accuracy would be so small, and the probability of error so great, that neither the one nor the other could be expressed arithmetically in figures. The calculation, in fact, would become lost in infinity. And

---

[1] I would not be understood as urging this. I presume the banquet at which the edict was issued took place on New Year's day. Nehemiah began to build the walls on the third day of the fifth month (Neh. vi. 15).   Ezra's journey from Babylon to Jerusalem occupied precisely four months (Ezra vii. 9), and in " the unchanging east" Nehemiah's journey from Susa would have occupied as long.   I conclude, therefore, that he set out in the *beginning* of Nisan.

this being so, any attempt to dismiss the facts
and figures set forth in the preceding chapter
as being accidental coincidences is not intelligent scepticism, but a crass misbelief which
is sheer credulity.

And this brings us back again to the
question, What is the character, and what
the credentials, of the book which contains
this most marvellous vision? The critics
themselves admit that the authority of the
Book of Daniel was unchallenged by Jews
and Christians alike for at least two thousand
years. It was not that the question of its
claims was never raised; for Porphyry the
Neo-Platonist devoted to the subject one of
his discourses against the Christians. But
Porphyry's attack evoked no response in
the Christian camp until modern German infidelity began its crusade against the Bible.
The visions of Daniel afforded an unanswerable testimony to the reality of inspiration, and their voice had to be silenced.
No matter to what date the 53rd chapter
of Isaiah be assigned, the sceptics would
reject the Messianic interpretation of it.

But if it can be proved that the visions of Daniel were written in the sixth century B.C., scepticism becomes an impossible attitude of mind.   Therefore, a propagandism designed to degrade the Bible to the level of a human book found it essential to prove that Daniel was written after the events it professed to predict.

To attain this end all the great erudition and patient subtlety for which German scholarship is justly famed, were prostituted without reserve ; and the attack of the apostates was an immense advance upon the attack of the Pagan. "Apostates," I say advisedly, for in its origin and purpose the movement was essentially anti-Christian. In course of time, however, men who had no sympathy with the aims of the rationalists were led to adopt their conclusions ; and in our own day the sinister origin of the movement is in danger of being forgotten. Its obtaining recruits among English scholars of repute is a matter within living memory.

First, then, we have the fact that the Book of Daniel, regarded as a classic, is a work of the very highest character, and that the attack upon it originated in the exigencies of modern rationalism. But secondly, the critics admit, for the fact is indisputable, that the Book of Daniel has entered more closely into the warp and woof of the New Testament than any other portion of the Hebrew Scriptures.[1] And if they do not admit as unreservedly that it comes to us expressly accredited by our Lord Himself, it is because the " Higher Criticism " is purely destructive, and therefore violates at times the principles on which all true criticism rests.[2] But whether they admit it or not, it is none the less certain. And as Keil justly says : " This testimony of our Lord fixes the seal of Divine confirmation on the external and internal evidences which prove the genuineness of the book."

And in view of these overwhelming proofs of its genuineness, if Hebrew scholars were

---

[1] See p. 68 ff., *ante*.

[2] In Matt. xxiv. 15, *e.g.*, there is no question of conflicting MSS. ; the words are admittedly quoted from Daniel, and the passage as a whole unmistakably refers to Daniel (see p. 70, *ante*).

agreed that its language was not that of the sixth century B.C., but of a later time, true criticism would seek for an explanation of that fact. But even those Hebraists who reject the book contradict one another on this very point ; and so Professor Driver falls back on the alleged presence of two Greek words in the text as settling the whole question. But in the circumstances this is but a travesty of true criticism, and proves nothing save the critic's want of practical experience in the art of sifting and weighing evidence.[1]

The case of the philologist having thus collapsed, the critic still further shakes our confidence in him by turning aside to borrow from the German rationalists a farrago of objections upon minor points. Some of these prove on inquiry to be either sheer blunders[2] or mere quibbles,[3] and most of them are so petty that no competent tribunal

---

[1] See pp. 51, 81, *ante*.

[2] *E.g.*, that Dan. i. 1 is unhistorical (see App. I., p. 153, *post*).

[3] *E.g.*, the spelling of " Nebuchadnezzar " (p. 45 *n. ante*), and that Belshazzar is called his son (p. 23, *ante*).

would listen to them, save in the absence of evidence worthy of the name.

If any should think that in my reply to Professor Driver I have treated these minor points of criticism too lightly, I would plead the advice once given by a great advocate, always to ignore the petty details of an opponent's evidence if his case can be shattered on some vital issue. There is not one of these difficulties and objections to which I have not given full and fair consideration, and a reply to them will be found in these pages.[1] But, I repeat, I am prepared to stake the whole case for Daniel on the two issues I have specified, namely, the inclusion of the book in the canon, and the fulfilment of its great central vision in Messianic times.

Behind these is the fact—which in itself ought to satisfy the Christian — that the book bears the express *imprimatur* of our Divine Lord. And we have the further

---

[1] To guard myself against any charge on this score, I give a summary of them in the Appendix. See Appendix VII., p. 179, *post*.

fact that its visions are inseparably interwoven with the Christian revelation and
with the whole scheme of unfulfilled prophecy. But this last topic I do not now
discuss. These pages are not addressed
to students of prophecy, for no student of
prophecy doubts the genuineness of Daniel.
But prophecy fulfilled has a voice for every
man ; and as Professor Driver's treatise is
addressed to men of the world from their
own standpoint,[1] I have here, waiving the
vantage ground of spiritual truth, appealed
to the judgment of all fair and reasonable
men.

Ptolemy the astronomer was a "Higher
Critic." The belief had long prevailed that

---

[1] I do not say this by way of complaint. Regarding the
Book of Daniel as no more than a classic, he treats it, of
course, on that footing. I recognise the difference between
what he has written on this subject and such productions,
e.g., as the article in Hastings' *Dictionary of the Bible*, of
which he is one of the editors ; or the article in Professor
Cheyne's rationalistic *Encyclopædia Biblica*. Were Porphyry the Pagan to come to life again he might without
reserve put his name to those articles, and to many another
article in both these works. If this is the sort of food sup-
plied to divinity students nowadays it is no wonder that so
many of them either lapse to rationalism or take refuge in
the superstitions of mere religion.

the sun was the centre of our system ; but he had no difficulty in proving that this traditional belief was untenable.   Once he got men to consider the matter from their own standpoint all could see the absurdity of supposing that the earth on which they lived and moved was flying helter-skelter round the sun.   And nothing more was needed but to keep the mind occupied with the many apparent difficulties of the hypothesis he opposed, to the exclusion of all thought of the few but insurmountable difficulties of the theory he advocated.   The professors and experts were convinced, the multitude followed suit, and for more than a thousand years the puerilities of the Ptolemaic System held sway, with the sanction of infallible science and the blessing of an infallible Church.

The allegory is a simple one.   There is a "Ptolemaic System" of studying the Bible, which is now struggling for supremacy. Let us, following the rationalists, insist on shutting out God, and dealing with the Bible from the purely human standpoint, and then we need but to weary our minds by the consideration of seeming difficulties of one kind, while we ignore overwhelming difficulties of another kind, and the victory of that false system will be assured. For the capacity of fairly considering both sides of a controversy is not common, and the habit of doing so is rare. Therefore it is that the best judge is not the legal expert, but the patient, broad-minded arbitrator, who will calmly hear both sides of a case, and then adjudicate upon it without prejudice or passion.

This brings me to my closing appeal; and I address it specially to those who are accustomed to take part in any capacity in the proceedings of our courts of justice. Once again, I ask them to remember that the question here at issue is essentially one for a judicial inquiry, and that if they possess experience of such inquiries their fitness for the task is greater than usually belongs to the professional scholar, however eminent. Philologists of high repute will tell them that the Book of Daniel is a forgery.   Other philologists of equal fame will assure them that it is genuine.   Let them set the opinion of the one set of experts against that of the other; and then, turning to consider the question on broader grounds, let them fearlessly decide it for themselves, uninfluenced by the glamour of great names.

The religious revolt of the sixteenth century rescued the Bible from the Priest: God grant that the twentieth century may bring a revolt which shall rescue it from the Professor and the pundit.

Appendices

Appendix 1
Nebuchadnezzar's First Invasion of Judea

THE opening statement of the Book of Daniel is here selected for special notice for two reasons. First, because the attack upon it would be serious, if sustained. And secondly and chiefly, because it is a typical specimen of the methods of the critics; and the inquiry may convince the reader of their unfitness to deal with any question of evidence. I am not here laying down the law, but seeking to afford materials to enable the reader to form his own opinion. *Ex uno disce omnes.*

Dan. i. 1 reads: "In the third year of the reign of Jehoiakim king of Judah came Nebuchadnezzar king of Babylon unto Jerusalem and besieged it." The German rationalists denounce this statement as a blunder. Their humble disciples, the English sceptics, accept their conclusion and blindly reproduce their arguments. Dr. Driver (*more suo*) takes a middle course and brands it as "doubtful" (*Daniel*, pp. xlviii and 2). I propose to show that the statement is historically accurate, and that its accuracy is established by the strict test of chronology.[1]

---

[1] For a complete and exhaustive analysis of the chronology I would refer to the "Chronological Treatise" in *The Coming Prince.*

A reference to Rawlinson's *Five Great Monarchies* (vol. iii. 488–494), and to Clinton's *Fasti Hellenici*, will show how thoroughly consistent the sacred history of this period appears to the mind of an historian or a chronologer, and how completely it harmonises with the history of Berosus. Jerusalem was first taken by the Chaldeans in the third year of Jehoiakim. His fourth year was current with the first year of Nebuchadnezzar (Jer. xxv. 1). This accords with the statement of Berosus that Nebuchadnezzar's first expedition took place before his actual accession (Josephus, *Apion*, i. 19). Then follows the statement quoted at p. 17, *ante*. But here we must distinguish between the narrative of Josephus, which is full of errors, and his quotation from Berosus, which is consistent and definite. Dr. Driver tells us that on this expedition, when Nebuchadnezzar reached Carchemish, he was confronted by the Egyptian army, and defeated it ; and that then, on hearing of his father's death, he hastened home *across the desert*. That German rationalists should have fallen into such a grotesque blunder as this, is proof of the blind malignity of their iconoclastic zeal : that English scholars should adopt it is proof that they have not brought an independent judgment to bear on this controversy. What Berosus says is that when Nebuchadnezzar heard of his father's death, " *he set the affairs of Egypt and the other countries in order*, and committed the captives he had taken *from the Jews*, and the Phœnicians, and

Syrians, and of the nations belonging to Egypt, to some of his friends . . . while he went in haste *over the desert* to Babylon." Will the critics tell us how he could have had Jewish captives if he had not invaded Judea ; how he could have reached Egypt without marching through Palestine ; how he could have returned to Babylon *over the desert* if he had set out from Carchemish on the Euphrates !

One error leads to another, and so Dr. Driver has to impugn also the accuracy of Jer. xlvi. 2 (which states that the battle of Carchemish was in Jehoiakim's fourth year), and further, to cook the chronology of Jehoiakim's reign by making his regnal years date from Tishri (p. xlix.)—a blunder that the *Mishna* exposes. (Treatise, *Rosh Hasha-nah*.) The regnal years of Jewish kings are always reckoned from Nisan.

According to the Canon of Ptolemy, the reign of Nebuchadnezzar dates from B.C. 604 : *i.e.* his accession was in the year beginning the 1st Thoth (which fell in January), B.C. 604. But the Captivity began in Nebuchadnezzar's eighth year (*cf.* Ezek. i. 2, and 2 Kings xxiv. 12) ; and in the thirty-seventh year of the Captivity Nebuchadnezzar's successor was on the throne (2 Kings xxv. 27). This, however, gives Nebuchadnezzar a reign of at least forty-four years, whereas according to the canon (and Berosus confirms it) he reigned only forty-three years. It follows, therefore, that Scripture antedates his reign and computes it from B.C. 605. (Clinton, *F. H.*, vol. i. p. 367.) This might be explained by the fact that the Jews acknowledged him as suzerain from that date. But it has been overlooked that it is accounted for by the *Mishna* rule of computing regnal years from Nisan to Nisan. In B.C. 604, the first Nisan fell on the 1st April, and according to the *Mishna* rule the king's second year would begin on that day, no matter how recently he had ascended the throne. Therefore the fourth year of Jehoiakim and the first year of Nebuchadnezzar (Jer. xxv. 1) was the year beginning Nisan B.C. 605 ; and the third year of Jehoiakim, in which Jerusalem was taken and the Servitude began, was the year beginning Nisan B.C. 606.

This result is confirmed by Clinton, who fixes the summer of B.C. 606 as the date of Nebuchadnezzar's first expedition. And it is strikingly confirmed also by a statement in Daniel which is the basis of one of the quibbles of the critics : Daniel was kept *three* years in training before he was admitted to the king's presence, and yet he interpreted the king's dream in his *second* year (Dan. i. 5, 18; ii. 1). The explanation is simple. While the Jews in Palestine computed Nebuchadnezzar's reign in their own way, Daniel, a citizen of Babylon and a courtier, of course accepted the reckoning in use around him. But as the prophet was exiled in B.C. 606, his three years' probation ended in B.C. 603, whereas the second year of Nebuchadnezzar, reckoned from his actual accession, extended to the early months of B.C. 602.

Again : the accession of Evil-Merodach was in

B.C. 561, and the thirty-seventh year of the Captivity was then current (2 Kings xxv. 27). Therefore the Captivity dated from the year Nisan 598 to Nisan 597. But this was (according to Jewish reckoning) the eighth year of Nebuchadnezzar (2 Kings xxiv. 12). His reign, therefore, dated from the year Nisan 605 to Nisan 604. And the first siege of Jerusalem and the beginning of the Servitude was in the preceding year, 606–605.

But seventy years was the appointed duration of the Servitude (*not* the Captivity, see p. 21, *ante*). And the Servitude ended in the first year of Cyrus, B.C. 536. *It must therefore have begun in* B.C. 606 (the third year of Jehoiakim), as the Book of Daniel records.

That date, therefore, is the pivot on which the whole chronology turns. On what ground then does Dr. Driver impugn it? Will it be believed that the only ground suggested is that 2 Kings xxiv. 1, which so definitely confirms Daniel, does not specify the particular year intended, and that Jeremiah xxv. and xxxvi. are silent with regard to the invasion of that year.

Let me examine this. I open Jer. xxv. to find these words: "The word that came to Jeremiah . . . in the fourth year of Jehoiakim . . . *that was the first year of Nebuchadrezzar, king of Babylon.*" Now Jeremiah had been a prophet for more than twenty years, yet till the fourth year of Jehoiakim he never mentions Nebuchadnezzar; but in that year he fixes a date by reference to his reign.

How is this to be explained ? The explanation is obvious, namely that by the capture of Jerusalem, the year before, as recorded in Dan. i. 1, and 2 Chron. xxxvi. 6, 7, Nebuchadnezzar had become suzerain. And yet Professor Driver tells us that " the invasion of Judea by Nebuchadnezzar, and the three years' submission of Jehoiakim, are certainly to be placed after Jehoiakim's fourth year—most probably indeed, towards the close of his reign " (*Daniel*, p. 2).

I now turn to Jer. xxxvi. This chapter records prophecies of the fourth and fifth year of Jehoiakim (vers. 1 and 9), and it is true that they do not mention an invasion before these years. But the critic has overlooked chapter xxxv. This chapter belongs to the same group as the chapter which follows it, and should of course be assigned to a date *not later* than the fourth year of the king. And in this chapter (verse 11) the presence of the Rechabites in Jerusalem is accounted for by the fact that Nebuchadnezzar's invasion had driven them from their homes. This chapter also thus affords signal confirmation of Daniel. The critics therefore hold, of course, that it belongs to the *close* of Jehoiakim's reign. And if we ask, Why should the history be turned upside down in this way ? they answer, Because the prophecies of the earlier years of his reign are silent as to this invasion ! This is a typical illustration of their logic and their methods.

I will only add that the silence of a witness is a

familiar problem with the man of affairs, who will sometimes account for it in a manner that may seem strange to the student at his desk. It may be due, not to ignorance of the event in question, but to the fact that that event was prominently present to the minds of all concerned.

Appendix 2

The Death of Belshazzar

THE following is Professor Sayce's rendering of the concluding (decipherable) portion of the Annalistic tablet of Cyrus:—

" On the fourteenth day of the month Sippara was taken without fighting; Nabonidos fled. On the sixteenth day Gobryas (Ugbaru), the Governor of the country of Kurdistan (Gutium), and the soldiers of Cyrus, entered Babylon without fighting. Afterwards Nabonidos was captured, after being bound in Babylon. At the end of the month Tammuz the javelin-throwers of the country of Kurdistan guarded the gates of E-Saggil; no cessation of services took place in E-Saggil ,and the other temples, but no special festival was observed. The third day of the month Marchesvan (October) Cyrus entered Babylon. Dissensions were allayed before him. Peace to the city did Cyrus establish, peace to all the province of Babylon did Gobryas his governor proclaim. Governors in Babylon he appointed. From the month Chisleu to the month Adar (November to February) the gods of the country of Accad, whom Nabonidos had transferred to Babylon, returned to their own cities. The eleventh day of the month Marchesvan, during the night, Gobryas was on the bank of the river.

. . . The wife of the king died. From the twenty-seventh day of Adar to the third day of Nisan there was lamentation in the country of Accad; all the people smote their heads. On the fourth day Kambyses the son of Cyrus conducted the burial at the temple of the Sceptre of the world. The priest of the temple of the Sceptre of Nebo, who upbears the sceptre [of Nebo in the temple of the god], in an Elamite robe took the hands of Nebo, . . . the son of the king (Kambyses) [offered] free-will offerings in full to ten times [the usual amount]. He confined to E-Saggil the [image] of Nebo. Victims before Bel to ten times [the usual amount he sacrificed]."

The reader's surprise will naturally be excited on learning that the tablet is so mutilated and defective that the text has here and there to be reconstructed, and that the above, while purporting to be merely a translation is, in fact, also a reconstruction. I will here confine myself, however, to one point of principal importance. Mr. Theo. G. Pinches, by whom this very tablet was first brought to light, is perfectly clear that the reading " the *wife* of the king died " cannot be sustained. He writes as follows [1] (I omit the cuneiform characters) :—

" Professor Sayce has adopted a suggestion of Professor Schrader. The characters cannot be . . .

---

[1] I wish to acknowledge my obligation to the Rev. John Urquhart, the author of *The Inspiration and Accuracy of the Holy Scriptures*, for placing this letter at my disposal.

' and the wife of,' but must be either . . . 'and ' (as I read it at first) or . . . 'and the son of.' This last improved reading I suggested about four years ago, and the Rev. C. J. Ball and Dr. Hagen, who examined the text with me, adopted this view. Dr. Hagen wrote upon the subject in Delitzsch's *Beiträge*, vol. i. Of course, whether we read 'and the king died,' or 'and the son of the king died,' it comes to the same thing, as either expression could refer to Belshazzar, who, after his father's flight, would naturally be at the head of affairs."

The following extract is from Mr. Pinches's article " Belshazzar " in the new edition of Smith's *Bible Dictionary* :—

" As is well known, Belshazzar was, according to Daniel v., killed in the night, and Xenophon (*Cyrop.*, vii. 5, 3) tells us that Babylon was taken by Cyrus during the night, whilst the inhabitants were engaged in feasting and revelry, and that the king was killed. So in the Babylonian Chronicle, lines 22–24, we have the statement that ' On the night of the 11th of Marchesvan, Ugbaru (Gobryas) [descended?] against [Babylon ?] and the king died. From the 27th of Adar until the 3rd of Nisan there was weeping in Akkad. All the people bowed their head.' The most doubtful character in the above extract is that which stands for the word 'and,' the character in question having been regarded as the *large group* which stands for that word. A close examination of the original, however, shows that it is possible that there are two characters instead of one—namely, the *small* character for 'and,' and the character *tur*, which in this connection would stand for *u mâr*, 'and the son of,' in which case the line would read, 'and *the son of* the king died.' Weeping in Akkad for Belshazzar is just what would be expected, when we take into consideration that he was for many years with the army there, and that he must have made himself a favourite by his liberality to the Akkadian temples. Even supposing, however, that the old reading is the right one, it is nevertheless possible that the passage refers to Belshazzar; for Berosus relates that Nabonidos, on surrendering to Cyrus, had his life spared, and that a principality or estate was given to him in Carmania, where he died. It is therefore at least probable that Belshazzar was regarded even by the Babylonians as king, especially after his father's surrender. With this improved reading of the Babylonian text, it is impossible to do otherwise than identify Gobryas with Darius the Mede (if we suppose that the last verse of the 5th chapter of Daniel really belongs to that chapter, and does not form part, as in the Hebrew text, of chap. vi.), he being mentioned, in the Babylonian Chronicle, in direct connection with the death of the king's son (or the king, as the case may be). This identification, though not without its difficulties, receives a certain amount of support from Daniel vi. 1, where it is stated that 'it pleased Darius to set over the kingdom an hundred and twenty princes,' &c.—an act which finds parallel in the Babylonian Chronicle, which states that, after Cyrus promised peace to Babylon, Gobryas, his governor, appointed governors in Babylon.'"

On this same subject I am indebted to Mr. St. Chad Boscawen for the following note :—

" Owing to the mutilated state of the latter part of the tablet, it is extremely difficult to arrange the events, and also in some cases to clearly understand the exact meanings of the sentences. As far as I can see, the course of events seems to have been as follows. Sippara was taken on the 14th of Tammuz, and two days later Babylon. Nabonidos had fled, but he was still recognised as king by the majority of the people, especially by rich trading communities such as the Egibi firm, who continued to date their contracts in his regnal years. At Sippara the people seem to have recognised Cyrus as king earlier than at Babylon, as the tablets of his accession year are *all*, with one exception, the source of which is not known, from Sippara. On the 3rd of Marchesvan Cyrus entered Babylon and appointed Gobryas (the prefect of Gutium) 'prefect of the prefects' (*pikhat-pikhate*) of Babylon; and he (Gobryas) appointed the *other prefects*. That reading of the sentence is perfectly legitimate. Cyrus seems only to have occupied himself with the restoration of religious order, and on restoring the gods to their temples who had been transported to Babylon. We have then a remarkable passage. Sayce reads 'the wife of the king died'; but Hagen reads the son of the king, and I have examined this tablet, and find that although the tablet is here broken, the most probable reading is . . . the *son*, not the *wife* . . .

"In Dan. v. we read, and 'Darius the Median took the kingdom, being about threescore and two years.' In a second passage, however, this is modified. We read, 'In the first year of Darius, the son of Ahasuerus, of the seed of the Medes, which was made king over the realm of the Chaldeans, (ix. 1); and again, 'It pleased Darius to set over the kingdom a hundred and twenty princes' (vi. 1). Here we have an exact parallel to the case of Gobryas. Gobryas was a Manda—among whom were embraced the Medes, for Astyages, an undoubted Median king, ruler of the Median capital of Ecbatana, is called . . . a soldier of the Manda, or barbarians. He is appointed on the 3rd Marchesvan B.C. 538— after taking the kingdom on 16th Tammuz—'prefect of the prefects '; and he appoints *other prefects* over the kingdom. His reign did not last more than one year, terminating in either Adar 538 or early in B.C. 537. The end is rendered obscure by the fractures in the tablet. . . .

"If, then, Gubaru or Gobryas was prefect of Gutium before his conquest of Babylon in B.C. 538, there is nothing whatever against his being a Mede; and as Astyages was deposed by a revolt, when 'he was taken by the hands of the rebels and given to Cyrus' (*Chronicle Inscr.*), it is very probable that Gobryas was the leader of the conspiracy. Indeed he seems to me to fulfil in every way the required conditions to be Darius the Mede. . . . The appointment of the satraps does not seem exorbitantly large, nor are these to be confounded with the satrapies of the Persian empire."

And finally, in his *Book of Daniel* (p. xxx) Professor Driver, in citing the foregoing extract from the tablet, reads the crucial sentence thus :—" On the 11th day of Marchesvan, during the night, Gubaru made an assault and *slew the king's son.*" And at pp. 60, 61 he writes: "After Gubaru and Cyrus had entered Babylon . . . he (Belshazzar) is said (according to the most probable reading) to have been slain by Gubaru 'during the night,' *i.e.* (apparently) in some assault made by night upon the fortress or palace to which he had withdrawn."

I will only add that, in view of the testimony of these witnesses, so thoroughly competent and impartial, it is not easy to restrain a feeling of indignation at the effrontery (not to use a stronger word) of Professor Sayce's language in pp. 525, 526 of his book.

Appendix 3
The Punctuation of Daniel 9:25

THE Massoretic punctuation of Daniel ix. 25 has been adopted by Dean Farrar and Professor Driver, who fail to see that it is fatal to their pseud-epigraph theory of Daniel. The passage when thus read limits to 62 "weeks" the period during which Jerusalem was to remain as an inhabited city; and it is quite certain that no Jew writing " in the days of the Seleucid tyrant, anxious to inspire the courage and console the sufferings of his countrymen," would have used words which could only mean that the destruction of their holy city was imminent. Assuming the genuineness of the Book of Daniel, the R.V. punctuation renders the meaning of the passage more obscure, but it cannot alter it ; for as $7+62+1$ make up 70, it is obvious that the lesser periods mentioned are subdivisions of the 70 weeks of the prophecy. It is clear, therefore, that the 62 weeks follow the 7 weeks, and that the death of Messiah (according to verse 26) was to be at the close of the 69th week.

"The sacred writings—Torah, Prophets, and Hagiographa—were written in archaic style, the

letters were unaccompanied by vowel or punctuation signs. . . . The accents and the vowel system
are an integral part of the Massorah."[1]   And
further, "The Received, or, as it is commonly
called, the Massoretic text of the Old Testament
Scriptures, has come down to us in manuscripts
which are of no very great antiquity, and which
all belong to the same family or recension" (Preface, R.V.). As the words "of no very great
antiquity" may be explained to mean not more
than about one thousand years old, the reader
can appreciate Professor Margoliouth's statement
"that we possess the Old Testament in a partially
anti-Christian recension."[2]   And as a false punctuation of Dan. ix. 25 would suffice to obscure, though
it could not destroy, the Messianic reference of the
passage, the Jewish editors may have possibly
sought in this way to lessen the weight of
proof which Daniel affords of the truth of Christianity.

But we may clear the Jewish editors from this
charge, though at the expense of the Old Testament
Company of Revisers. Punctuation marks (as we
understand the term) there are none in Hebrew.
But the Hebrew *accents* serve to a certain extent the
same purpose. The following extract from the
Gesenius-Kautzsch *Hebrew Grammar*[3] (than which

---

[1] *The Hebrew Accents*, by Arthur Davis.   (Myers & Co.,
1900.)

[2] *Lines of Defence*, p. 242.

[3] Clarendon Press, 1898 (p. 56).

there is no higher authority) will enable the reader to judge of this matter for himself:—

"The design of the accents is *primarily* to regulate the musical enunciation (chanting) of the sacred Text; and thus they are first of all a kind of musical notes. . . . On the other hand, according to their original design they have also a twofold use which is still of the greatest importance for the grammar—viz., their value (a) *as marking the tone;* (b) *as marks of punctuation*." And to this a footnote is added to explain "that the value of the accent as a mark of punctuation is always relative. Thus, *e.g.*, 'Athnâh, as regards the logical structure of the sentence, may at one time indicate a very strong cæsure (thus Gen. i. 4); at another, one which is almost imperceptible (thus Gen. i. 1)."

Now it is the presence of the Athnah accent which has led the Revisers to divide Dan. ix. 25 by a colon. On the same principle and for the same reason they ought to have rendered Gen. i. 1, "In the beginning God created: the heaven and the earth." In the Hebrew the order of the words is, "In the beginning created God;" and the force of the Athnah is to make the reader pause at the sacred name in order that the hearers may grasp the solemn meaning of the words. In every case, therefore, the context must decide whether the accent should be "translated" by the insertion of a colon in the English version. The Revisers, however, by a majority vote, and in spite of the protest of the American Company, have thus corrupted Dan. ix. 25. It is one of the blemishes of the

R.V. of the Old Testament, which is generally free from these "schoolboy translations,"[1] that so often mark the R.V. of the New Testament. I will conclude by repeating that if their punctuation here is right, it is proof that Daniel was not written in the Maccabean era.

Since writing the foregoing my attention has been called to the presence of the Athnah in verse 2 of this very chapter. If the critics are right they ought to render it, "I, Daniel, understood by the books: the number of the years, &c." But their position is in fact utterly untenable.

---

[1] Eccles. xii. 5 is a notable instance of this. The beautifully veiled reference implied in the caper-berry is rendered with exquisite propriety in our A.V., "and desire shall fail." The R.V. reading, "and the caper-berry shall fail," is a mere schoolboy translation, and absolutely meaningless to the English reader.

Appendix 4

The Jewish Calendar

ACCORDING to the *Mishna* (treatise *Rosh Hashanah*), "On the 1st of Nisan is a new year for the computation of the reign of kings and for festivals." To which the Jewish editors of the English translation of the *Mishna* add this note: "The reign of Jewish kings, whatever the period of accession might be, was always reckoned from the preceding Nisan; so that if, for instance, a Jewish king began to reign in Adar, the following month (Nisan) would be considered as the commencement of the second year of his reign. This rule was observed in all legal contracts, in which the reign of kings was always mentioned." This rule, I may add, will explain what Christian expositors and critics are pleased to call the "errors" in the chronological statements of Scripture as to Jewish regnal years.

Full information on the subject of the present Jewish year will be found in Lindo's *Jewish Calendar*, and in the *Encyc. Brit.*, 9th ed., article "Hebrew Calendar." But while their calendar is now settled with astronomical accuracy, it was not so in early times. And nothing is certainly known of the embolismal system then in use, to adjust the lunar to the solar year. But the testimony of the *Mishna* is definite that the great characteristic of the sacred year, as ordained in the Mosaic age, remained unchanged in Messianic times; namely, it began with the first appearance of the Paschal moon. The *Mishna* states that the Sanhedrim required the evidence of two competent witnesses that they had *seen* the new moon. The rules for the journey and examination of the witnesses contemplate the case of their coming from a distance, and being "a night and a day on the road." The proclamation by the Sanhedrim may therefore have been delayed for a day or two after the phasis, and the phasis may sometimes have been delayed till the moon was 1 d. 17 h. old. So that the 1st Nisan may sometimes have fallen several days later than the true new moon. (See Clinton, *Fasti Rom.*, vol. ii. p. 240.)

All writers therefore who, *e.g.*, fix the date of the Crucifixion by assigning it to a year in which the Paschal full moon was on a Friday, are clearly wrong. The elements of doubt are: (1) The time of the phasis; (2) the appearance of the necessary witnesses; (3) the rules to prevent the festivals falling on unsuitable days; and (4) the embolismal system in force, of which we know nothing certainly. The use of the Metonic cycle in settling the Jewish calendar dates only from the fourth century A.D.; and as the old eight years' cycle was in use among the early Christians for settling Easter, the presumption is that it was borrowed from the Jews.

Let me illustrate this by A.D. 32, the year which Scripture itself marks out as the year of the Crucifixion. The true new moon was late on the night (10 h. 57 m.) of the 29th March. The proclamation of the Sanhedrim therefore would naturally have occurred on the 31st. But, as above explained, it may have been delayed till 1st April; and in that case the 15th Nisan should have fallen on Tuesday the 15th April. But according to the scheme of the eight years' cycle, the embolismal month was inserted in the 3rd, 6th, and 8th years; and an examination of the calendars from A.D. 22 to 45 will show that A.D. 32 was the 3rd year of such a cycle. And as the difference between the solar year and the lunar is 11¼ days, it would amount in three years to 33¾ days, and the addition of a 13th month (*Ve-Adar*) of 30 days would leave an epoch still remaining of 3¾ days. And the "ecclesiastical moon" being that much before the real moon, the Passover festival would have fallen on Friday (11th April). I have dealt with this question at greater length in *The Coming Prince*, pp. 99–105.

Appendix 5

The Twentieth Year of Artaxerxes

THE month Nisan in the twentieth year of Artaxerxes is the epoch of the prophetic era of the seventy weeks. In dealing with this subject, therefore, it is of vital importance to fix that date, and I have dealt with the matter exhaustively in an *Excursus* (App. II., Note A) added to *The Coming Prince*, to which I beg leave to refer the reader. I will here give but one extract :—

"According to Clinton (*F. H.*, vol. ii. p. 380), the death of Xerxes was in July, B.C. 465, and the accession of Artaxerxes was in February, B.C. 464. Artaxerxes, of course, ignored the usurper's reign, which intervened, and reckoned his own reign from the day of his father's death. Again, of course, Nehemiah, being an officer of the court, followed the same reckoning. Had he computed his master's reign from February 464, Chislen and Nisan could not have fallen in the same regnal year (Neh. i. 1 ; ii. 1). No more could they, had he, according to Jewish practice, computed it from Nisan."

Not content, however, with my own investigations, I appealed to the author of *The Five Great Monarchies*, and Canon Rawlinson favoured me with the following reply: "You may safely say that chronologers are now agreed that Xerxes died in the year B.C. 465. The Canon of Ptolemy, Thucidides, Diodorus, and Manetho are agreed, the only counter authority being Ctesias, who is quite untrustworthy."

Then as regards the Julian date of the 1st Nisan, B.C. 445 (Neh. ii.), when my book was in the press, I began to fear lest my own lunar calculations to fix the Jewish New Year (see Appendix IV., *ante*), might prove untrustworthy, and accordingly I wrote to the then Astronomer-Royal, Sir George Airy, who replied as follows: "I have had the moon's place calculated from Largeteau's Tables in additions to the *Connaisance des Temps*, 1846, by one of my assistants, and have no doubt of its correctness. The place being calculated for —444, March 12 d. 20 h., French reckoning, or March 12 d. 8 h. P.M., it appears that the said time was short of New Moon by about 8 h. 47 m., and therefore the New Moon occurred at 4 h. 47 m. A.M., March 13th, Paris time."

The New Moon, therefore, occurred at Jerusalem on the 13th March, B.C. 445 (—444 Astronomical) at 7 h. 9 m. A.M. And the next day, the 14th, was the 1st Nisan.

Appendix 6
The Date of the Crucifixion

As regards the date of the Ministry and of the Passion, Luke iii. 1 is an end of controversy with all who reject the nightmare system of interpreting Scripture. The 15th year of the Emperor Tiberius is as certain a date as the 15th year of Queen Victoria. He began to reign on the 19th August A.D. 14. "And no single case has ever been, or can be, produced in which the years of Tiberius were reckoned in any other manner."

But Gibbon tells us that "The Roman Emperors . . . invested their designed successor with so large a share of present power as should enable him, after their decease, to assume the remainder without suffering the empire to perceive the change of masters. Thus Augustus . . . obtained for his adopted son [Tiberius] the censorial and tribunitian power, and dictated a law by which the future prince was invested with an authority equal to his own over the provinces and the armies. Thus Vespasian . . . associated Titus to the full powers of the Imperial dignity" (*Decline and Fall*, I. ch. 3).

And this is made an excuse for "cooking" the chronology by those who, in spite of the clear testimony of Scripture, insist on assigning the Crucifixion to A.D. 29 or 30. They treat the reign of Tiberius as beginning some years before the death of Augustus, and take his 15th year to mean his 12th year. Sanclementi, indeed, finding "that nowhere in his time, or on monuments or coins, is a vestige to be found of any such mode of reckoning the years of this emperor," disposes of the difficulty by taking the date in Luke iii. 1 to refer to the Passion! Browne adopts this in a modified form. He says "it is improbable to the last degree" that Luke, who wrote specially for a Roman officer, and generally for Gentiles, would have so expressed himself as to be certainly misunderstood by them. Therefore, though the statement of the Evangelist clashes with his date for the Passion, he owns his obligation to accept it. (See *Ordo Sæc.*, §§ 71 and 75.)

The Evangelist's chronology refutes the traditional date embodied in the spurious *Acta Pilati* formerly quoted in this controversy, and in the writings of certain of the Fathers — "by some because they confounded the date of the baptism with the date of the Passion; by others, because they supposed both to have happened in one year; by others, because they transcribed from their predecessors without examination" (Fynes Clinton, *Fasti Rom.*, A.D. 29).

The advocates of this false chronology rely, first, on a wrong inference from the Evangelist's statement that the Lord "when He began (to teach) was about thirty years of age" (Luke iii. 23). But, as Alford says, this "admits of considerable latitude, *but only in one direction*, viz. *over* thirty years." And, secondly, on the figment that the Passion must have occurred in a year when the Paschal moon was full upon a Friday. But this is a blunder. John xviii. 3 makes it clear that the Passover of the Crucifixion was *not* at the full moon. For in that case there would have been no "lanterns and torches," especially having regard to Luke xxii. 2. See Appendix IV. (p. 172 *f. ante*); and also Clinton's *Fasti Rom.*, vol. ii. p. 240, as to the impossibility of determining in what year the Passover fell on a Friday. The whole question is dealt with fully in *The Coming Prince*, ch. viii.

Appendix 7

Professor Driver's
Indictment of Daniel

THE following is a brief summary of Professor Driver's indictment of the Book of Daniel.

He enumerates under nine heads "facts of a historical nature" which point to an author later than Daniel (pp. xlvii–lvi). These are :—

1. The position of the Book in the Jewish Canon. (As to this see pp. 57–61, and 103–108, *ante.*)

2. The omission of his name from Ecclesiasticus. (See pp. 57, 98 *n.*, *ante.*)

3. That the Book of Kings is silent as to the siege mentioned in Dan. i. 1. (See p. 15 and App. I., *ante.*)

4. The use of the term "Chaldean." (See p. 45 *n.*, *ante.*)

5. That Belshazzar is spoken of as king, and as son of Nebuchadnezzar. (See p. 23 *ff.*, *ante.*)

6. The mention of Darius the Mede as King of Babylon. (See p. 31 *ff.* and 165, *ante.*)

7. The mention of "the books" in Dan. ix. 2. The word *sepher* means simply a scroll. It often denotes a *book ;* often a letter (as, *e.g.*, Jer. xxix. 1, or Isa. xxxvii. 14.) Then again Jer. xxxvi. 1, 2 records that Jeremiah's prophecies up to that time

were recorded in a "book." And ten years later a further "book" of them was sent to Babylon (Jer. li. 60, 61). Or if any one insists that "the books" must here mean a recognised canon, where is the difficulty? The statement that no such "collection" existed in B.C. 536 is one of those wanton assertions that abound in this controversy. It may "safely be affirmed" with certainty that the scrolls of the Law were kept together. And there was no man on earth more likely to possess them than the great prophet-prince of the Captivity.

8. "The incorrect explanation of the name Belteshazzar in iv. 8." (As Dr. Driver goes on to describe this as "doubtful" (p. liv.), I have not deemed it necessary to notice it.)

9. The "improbability" that strict Jews would have accepted a position among the "wise men" (see p. 13, *ante*), and other like "improbabilities." (As Dr. Driver goes on to admit that these do not possess weight, and "should be used with reserve," I have not dwelt upon them.)

His second ground of attack is the language of the book (lvi.–lxiii.). This has been fully discussed in these pages (ch. iv.).

And the third ground is "the theology of the book." After deprecating the "exaggerations of the rationalists" under this head, he proceeds:—
"It is undeniable that the conception of the future Kingdom of God, and the doctrines of angels, of the resurrection, and of a judgment on the world, appear in Daniel in a more developed form than elsewhere

in the Old Testament." Far be it from me to deny
it! It is largely on this very account that the
Christian values the book, remembering as he does,
what Professor Driver ignores, that its teaching in
all these respects is definitely adopted and developed
in the New Testament. And if he finds that the
later Jewish apocalyptical literature resembles the
book in some respects, he has no difficulty in
accounting for the resemblance. (See p. 57, *ante.*)

I make the critic a present of the entire argument
under this head of " the theology of the book," save
on three points. And they are points which would
never have been urged by an English Christian
writer save under the influence of German infidelity.

1. It is not true that the interest of the book *culminates* in the history of Antiochus. As all Christian
expositors with united voice maintain, it culminates
in the prophecy of Messiah's advent and death.
And as all students of prophecy recognise, it reaches
on to the time of the ğreat Antichrist of whom
Antiochus was but a type.

2. Daniel's passionately earnest prayer recorded
in ch. ix. is a complete answer to the statement that
he took "little interest in the welfare and prospects
of his contemporaries."

3. We are told that "the minuteness of the predictions embracing even special events in the distant
future, is also out of harmony with the analogy of
prophecy." If this were sustained it would not affect
the book as a whole, but serve merely to accredit the
suggestion urged by some writers that part of chap. xi.

is an interpolation. But in view of the facts this allegation is as strange as that under (2) *supra*, and as many others in Professor Driver's book. What about the minute predictions scattered through the Old Testament respecting the Nativity and the Passion ? And the last eight chapters of Ezekiel contain a mass of predictions which still await fulfilment, as minute as anything in Daniel.

This is all that the Higher Criticism has to urge against the Book of Daniel.

Index

Other Titles by Sir Robert Anderson

THE COMING PRINCE

This is the standard work on the marvelous prophecy of Daniel about the antichrist and the "seventy weeks". It deals fully with the details of the chronology and with the vexing questions of the last of the "seventy sevens".

ISBN 0-8254-2115-2   384 pp.   paperback

FORGOTTEN TRUTHS

The author shares valuable answers to the questions resulting from the delay of our Lord's return, as well as other seemingly irreconcilable truths.

ISBN 0-8254-2130-6   166 pp.   paperback

THE GOSPEL AND ITS MINISTRY

A study of such basic Christian truths as Grace, Reconcilation, Justification, and Sanctification. In the author's own direct, yet devotional, style, these truths are presented in such a way that the skeptic becomes convinced and the believer is edified.

ISBN 0-8254-2126-8   224 pp.   paperback

THE LORD FROM HEAVEN

A devotional treatment of the doctrine of the deity of Christ, offering the testimony of the Scriptures as to its validity. This book is not written to settle doctrinal controversy, but rather it is a practical Bible study that will deepen the student's conviction.

ISBN 0-8254-2127-6   120 pp.   paperback

REDEMPTION TRUTHS

The author presents unique insights on the gift offer of salvation, the glory of sonship, and the grandeur of eternity's splendor.

ISBN 0-8254-2131-4   192 pp.   paperback

THE SILENCE OF GOD

If God really cares, why has He let millions on earth suffer, starve, and fall prey to the ravages of nature? Why has He been silent for nearly 2,000 years? The author gives a thorough and Scriptural answer. He also discusses the subject of miracles today with excellent answers. Here is a "must read" book for the serious Bible student.

ISBN 0-8254-2128-4   232 pp.   paperback

TYPES IN HEBREWS

A study of the types found in the book of Hebrews. Anderson ties the revelation of God to the Hebrew nation with the full revelation to the Church of Jesus Christ. The premise is that God's provision for the Jews represented the future blessings for Christians. The author augments his insights with the comments of other Bible scholars.

ISBN 0-8254-2129-2   192 pp.   paperback

Available at your local Christian bookseller, or:

KREGEL Publications

P. O. Box 2607 • Grand Rapids, MI 49501-2607